W9-CBL-275

THE NEW YORK TIMES
BOOK OF INTERIOR DESIGN
AND DECORATION

THE NEW YORK TIMES BOOK OF INTERIOR DESIGN AND DECORATION

NORMA SKURKA

NYT Times BOOKS

Copyright © 1976 by Norma Skurka. All rights reserved, including the right
to reproduce this book or portions thereof in any form.

For information, address: Quadrangle/The New York Times Book Co., Inc.,
Three Park Avenue, New York, New York 10016

Manufactured in the United States of America.

Published simultaneously in Canada by Optimum Publishing Company
Limited, Montreal.

Book design: Paul Hanson

Library of Congress Cataloging in Publication Data

Skurka, Norma.
        The New York times book of interior design and
decoration.

        Bibliography: p.
        Includes index.
        1. Interior decoration—United States.   2. Interior decoration—
Europe.   I. Title.
NK2004.S57   1976   747′.8′83   76–9690
ISBN 0–8129–0653–5

*A picture is worth
a thousand words.*

Old Chinese Proverb

Pictures tell the story of decorating more vividly than words. My thanks, then, to all the photographers who lent their work for this book, especially to Norman McGrath, Richard Champion, James Mathews, Robert Perron, Peter Reed, Jeremiah Bragstad, Carla de Benedetti, Emmett Bright—superb technicians all and gifted with a sensitive eye. I also wish to thank the designers for freely contributing their thoughts and experiences on the mystique-shrouded subject of design.

The late Rose Cumming in her famous Park Avenue shop.

PHOTO: JAMES MATHEWS

CONTENTS

INTRODUCTION

To be happy at home is the ultimate result of all ambition, the end to which every enterprise and labor tends. . . .
Samuel Johnson

This penthouse apartment in Manhattan enjoys the best of both worlds, old and new, in the way it is furnished with an antique chaise longue, porcelain stove, harpsichord, and modern art. The marble flooring was salvaged from the Hotel Pierre ballroom, where owner Mimi Howells danced as a young girl.
PHOTO: NORMAN MCGRATH

WE ALL WANT TO LIVE in beautiful surroundings. Even primitive man, once he had gained control over his environment, turned his cooking pots and textiles into things of beauty. Our homes are infinitely more than mere shelters. It isn't enough that a habitation be functional; otherwise we would be content with the hospital or motel room.

A home symbolizes our hopes, desires, and sense of accomplishment. If we have satisfied these goals, it will show up in our surroundings. We seek a place that gives pleasure, a place where we can relax, feel happy, and be content. Whether it is a rambling mansion or a one-room apartment, it is home base, our central reference point vis-à-vis the rest of the world. It is the one place where we are in control.

We don't think of our homes as being independent of or separate from ourselves. They are a part of us, an expression of our own identity. Since a home is usually the family seat and center of domestic life, we are surrounded not only by objects we cherish but by those persons whom we love most in the world. A family needs a home for physical comfort, spiritual renewal and refreshment; it is a place where we can recharge our batteries before facing the world. We require a sense of familiarity and belonging, an environment where people and objects are a part of us. Children gain their standards of behavior at home, standards which they carry with them throughout their lives.

Mere functionalism is definitely not enough to make a house a home. We want efficient shelter, certainly, but we also want an environment that is inviting, soothing yet stimulating, intimate yet not confining, personal yet orderly. Such a harmonious diversity is the goal of all successful interior design. The spirit or atmosphere that suffuses our home is as important as the practical objects used to furnish it.

Decoration and design are both elements that can elevate a home above the commonplace. It is one thing to furnish a house and quite another to imbue it with a sense of style. Cecil Beaton, the noted photographer and set designer, tried to define that elusive quality when he wrote: "Most of us, according to our means, imprint our personality upon our surroundings. It is a human and beneficial thing to do for it is this tendency that has led to the creation of many rooms which give happiness. It is nearly always the personal that inspires and delights us. There may be only a knife-edge difference between a room that is alive and one that has no soul."

What Beaton was saying, in essence, is that creating a beautiful home doesn't depend upon money or even on the amount of space available. It is really a question of one's frame of mind. It mirrors a positive attitude, a joie de vivre. It is merely the accumulation of hundreds of everyday decisions about how we want to live. How much does it cost to place a bud vase on the breakfast table or to hang all the pots and pans near the stove so that they're ready when the desire hits you to make that wonderful soup or omelette? People who live full, rich lives tend to build pleasurable, harmonious surroundings. Unpleasant places too often reflect a dreary, gloomy outlook on life.

Is this, then, what decorating is all about? Decorating has always been synonymous with the art of living well. It began as a formal profession in the seventeenth century, a time of great activity in all the building arts. Before then, there was no significant division of labor among the arts of architecture, sculpture, painting, and decoration. Artists designed the buildings and also embellished the interiors. A cultured patron knew enough about architecture to design his own manor house or, at the very least, to be on comfortable ground with his architect. It was required of every gentleman that he be conversant with the rules governing architecture and that he take pride in the minutest details of the house and its furnishings. We can find traces of this tradition in early America: George Washington remodeled and redesigned Mount Vernon; Thomas Jefferson designed his own residence, Monticello, as well as numerous other public buildings, including the University of Virginia.

From the seventeenth century onwards, Europe's aristocrats spared no expense to build splendid mansions and châteaux; they hired the best professionals they could afford. This gradually gave rise to the decorative heritage that still influences today's interiors. Furniture which we call Louis XV, Georgian, French Provincial, Chippendale, and Empire were among the great styles with which these mansions were furnished. Our present-day versions resemble these noble ancestors only slightly. (More on the subject of debased style will be found in the next chapter.)

It's absurd to transplant the lifestyles of that bygone aristocratic age to the boxlike rooms of the high-rise apartment or the split-level ranch in the suburbs. Yet people still try to do just that. More liberal social attitudes, changing living patterns, greater mobility, advanced technology, and lack of servants—all indicate that times have changed. Adopting the stiff and stilted manners of court life would be as ludicrous as parading around in old-fashioned costumes. Retinues of servants are a thing of the past; conversely, central vacuum cleaners, dishwashers, and refrigerators were unknown a century or so ago.

The first real distinction between an old-fashioned and a new piece of furniture involved a stripping away of all elements which did not aid and enhance its function. Did the curved leg of a chair make it more comfortable, more resilient? If not, the leg was straightened. Was wood truly the most economical material for the chair frame or for the table top? It might, perhaps, be replaced by a material like glass or plastic. Did the sofa need to be filled with expensive down and have an elaborately carved frame to be efficient for seating purposes? Soon sofas with skinny steel legs and tufted leather backs appeared.

Such furniture, called "functional," looked radically different from anything which had previously been designed. Today, we call it "modern."

At about the same time, the house shell was being reanalyzed for efficiency, practicality, and functionalism. The streamlined quality of furniture, moreover, merely echoed the lines of architecture. Houses designed by such innovative architects of the time as Le Corbusier, Mies van der Rohe, Frank Lloyd Wright, and Walter Gropius were stripped down to skin and bones—sleek geometric shapes. Functionalism underlined the form and was immediately apparent from its appearance.

Such was the state of the arts during the first decades of the twentieth century. Changing lifestyles are always reflected in interior design and architecture. And changes are still going on. In the past twenty-five years, servants have increasingly become a luxury. The woman of the house usually does the cooking and serving, while dad may wind up doing the dishes. The concept of the dining room as a stiff and formal place, isolated from the kitchen, is disappearing; it is now part of the kitchen—or opens up into it. The kitchen is no longer hidden away at the back of the house along with the cooking odors; it is the house's hub, the center of activity. The bathroom, too, is larger, more sybaritic, and, where money permits, has a dressing area and sauna or exercise room. The bedroom and bathroom are merging into one rejuvenating environment.

Our rare moments of relaxation are precious in today's pressured world. We want more comfort, more nonchalance in our living environment. We want a house that takes care of us rather than our having to take care of it. As life becomes more complex, we want our home to be more inviting, more sheltering, more satisfying. Today's interiors are havens of informality, comfort, easy care, efficiency, practicality. They can also be beautiful.

Gradually disappearing is the cold, austere interior for which modern design was criticized. Today's interiors are softened by rich, natural materials and textures, and by flexible atmospheric lighting. Spatial arrangements are seriously thought out and the uncluttered effect is desired. There is less of a need for garish colors and patterns, for tabletops of objects and other phony status symbols. Space and light today stand on their own merits.

THE QUESTION OF STYLE

There is nothing quite so boring as false refinement or so vulgar as misplaced elegance.
Billy Baldwin

ROOMS SAY A GREAT DEAL about their occupants. What we choose to live with reflects our educational, ethnic, and social background, our age, and our economic and cultural development. The furniture we select, its quality and style, the art work and the harmony or discord of the overall effect transmits this subtle information. Rooms are the clues to where we stand at a given moment of our lives. They speak silently about how we think, what we value, and who we are.

The worst mistake that people can make is to turn their rooms into advertisements of themselves. They want their rooms to confirm social status and wealth. They stuff the space with pretentious, stiff furniture selected not because they like it but because it is expensive and may impress others. Nobody is fooled. The approach destroys a person's self-identity and creative talents. It turns the personality into a rude caricature. The room that has the simplest things in it is often the most elegant place in town.

The villain behind all this is the fact that people confuse good taste with great expense. Taste is an abstraction that has no exact meaning. Yesterday's good taste becomes today's folly. Style is another difficult word to define. It embraces a design totality: structural integrity, suitability of purpose, efficiency of function, economy of materials, appropriateness, and, of course, beauty.

Style, in the historic sense, refers to a time when architecture and furniture carried a characteristic design. We refer to such styles as Louis XV, English Chippendale, American Empire—to name just a few. (There are, of course, many other styles; a capsule history of the most important ones is provided in the next chapter.) The style that most of us are familiar with is no longer a pure reflection of the historic style that inspired it.

The question of style troubles us because we feel obligated to "choose a style" for the furniture in our homes. Yet few of us have escaped a steady diet of misinformation about style. It begins with the houses we live in.

Houses put up by speculative builders are packaged in a mass-market version of style. Some of the more popular ones are labeled Colonial, French Provincial, Mediterranean, and Swiss Chalet. The front door of the house usually has a pastiche of decorative architecture: a pedimental doorway for Colonial; wrought ironwork for Mediterranean; bay windows and mansard roof for French Provincial; and

Designers David Easton and Michael La Rocca used the hallway that links the front and back rooms of a townhouse to advantage as a bed alcove and also as a place to store books.
PHOTO: RICHARD CHAMPION

15

Furniture runs the gamut from modern seating and cocktail table to traditional console and porcelains in the living room of designers Jay Hyde Crawford and Anthony Tortora.
PHOTO: PAUL VANEYRE

gingerbread trim for Swiss Chalet. Behind these thin disguises is the same, ordinary house.

And where do we get our ideas about furniture styles? At the department store. It, too, has a shorthand version of style. The bridal salon, painted pale blue and furnished with French Provincial furniture, is translated into the master bedroom after marriage and perpetuated in the little girl's room. The den or library is a reproduction of the haberdashery section of the department store. The dark paneling and plaid carpet is supposed to look like a men's club or the library of a Scottish castle. The kitchen is Colonial with knotty pine cabinets. The dining room is always Chippendale.

That is the way designer John Saladino described the stylistic parody of most of our homes. It's like people living in containers and being given container-packaged ideas, like "going to the supermarket and picking up a can of French Provincial and a box of Chippendale," according to Saladino.

Because style has been subjected to gross corruption, very little of what is called "style" has anything to do with it. Still, people continue to struggle with the question of choosing furniture in a particular style or, even more significant, with the biggest question of all: modern versus traditional?

Unless a house is furnished exclusively with antiques, all of the furniture we select, regardless of the name tag, is modern furniture. It is "made today" in manufacture if not in style. The tools used, the materials, the construction, the decoration—all are contemporary. Even if it is a good reproduction, the piece of furniture would never be confused with a real antique.

The same is true of our rooms. We live in modern rooms. They can be studiously decorated to resemble the past, furnished with antiques appropriate to the period, but they are twentieth-century habitats. The fabrics will probably be easy-care synthetics rather than fragile silks and damasks. The surfaces on counters and floors will be washable or protected by stainproof coatings. The lighting will not be gaslight or candlelight but electricity, and the room will have electrical outlets and contemporary light fixtures. No one really wants to return to the discomforts of another age—inadequate heating, no indoor plumbing, and no running water. The truly traditional rooms exist only in museums. The real question about choosing furniture is: how "modern" do you want your modern rooms to be?

The next chapter presents a capsule history of furniture styles. Learning how styles developed is the best clue to selecting one to live with.

A SHORT HISTORY
OF FURNITURE

I N MEDIEVAL TIMES, furniture hardly existed in the Western world. The precious little that did exist was more-or-less identical in all countries. Medieval castles were stone fortresses whose main function was to keep out the marauding enemy rather than provide for an occupant's comfort. (Windows, for example, were mere arrow slits.) A typical household inventory included a few simple chests (the drawer had not yet been invented), stools, and settle benches. Tables consisted of huge boards temporarily laid across trestle bases and dismantled after meals. Chairs were stiff-backed, not upholstered, and consequently uncomfortable, reserved expressly for the lord of the manor.

Furniture forms evolved only gradually. The simple chest or trunk of planks and heavy boards first developed a separate stand and subsequently was constructed with legs. Once the box was off the floor and up on legs, it was modified to accommodate hinged doors that opened from the front and, finally, a drawer. Cupboards and benches were originally part of the architecture of the room; even when they were made to stand free of the walls, they were still massive, heavy, and immobile.

Furniture design advanced beyond rude medieval forms during the Italian Renaissance in the fifteenth century, a time of great flowering of all the arts, but did not gain much in simple comfort. Tall cupboards and massive chests were embellished with all sorts of architectural details—columns, pediments, moldings, statuettes—usually found on buildings rather than furniture. The Renaissance marked the beginning of an architectural and decorative style called *baroque*.

The Renaissance developed in Italy, an important banking, mercantile, and shipping crossroads between the East and the West, one which was also heir to the Roman Empire and seat of the Western Roman Church. Surrounded by the ruins of antiquity, Italian scholars turned their study to texts of ancient Greece and Rome. This investigation led to the rediscovery and appreciation of much forgotten knowledge which, in turn, resulted in a flourishing of all the decorative arts —painting, furniture, architecture, and domestic design based on antique or "classic" ideals.

Although the Renaissance added little to furniture comfort, it changed the face of furniture design when it was imported into France by Louis XIV in the seventeenth century.

A magnificent English antique secretary is surfaced with burl wood veneer; it has a segmental arch top and is adorned with pilasters flanking the bookshelves.
PHOTO: TOM WIER

19

FRENCH STYLES

French design is dominated by the names of three monarchs: Louis XIV (1638–1715), Louis XV (1710–1774), and Louis XVI (1754–1793). Court styles were designed solely to express the glory of the monarch and to adorn his palaces; as such, they were exceedingly ornate and elaborate. Louis XIV was dubbed "The Sun King" because of his lavish expenditures on his court and palaces, especially Versailles, which he built in a marshy forest twelve miles west of Paris. Even today, Versailles looms as the zenith of the French baroque style —everything about it is colossal in scale, magnificent in concept, and pompous in character. Louis XIV's court at Versailles set the standard of excellence for all other European courts of the time.

Baroque style, which almost bankrupted the French state because of the excessive taxation needed to finance its lavishness, ended with the death of Louis XIV in 1715. The nation was ruled by a regent until the successor, Louis XV, the King's five-year-old great-grandson, reached his majority. During this brief interlude of roughly thirty

The staircase landing of this apartment designed by Denning and Fourcade serves as a dining area with French Louis XVI chairs and an eighteenth-century commode.
PHOTO: NORMAN MCGRATH

years, a transitional furniture style called *Régence* came into fashion (1700–1740). Some connoisseurs consider the Régence style to be finer than the styles immediately preceding and following it; Régence skirts the extreme grandeur of Louis XIV and avoids the effeminacy of Louis XV. (Because of its courtliness, baroque styling is unsuited to modern-day living; examples of it, either antiques or reproductions, are rarely encountered outside of museums. One rarely encounters a gilded console table or mirror in baroque styling, while one can still find Régence, Louis XV and Louis XVI, the succeeding styles, popular as antiques and in reproduction form.)

French Régence is not to be confused with the English Regency style; they are two distinct periods that bear no relationship to each other. Régence furniture, unlike its baroque predecessor, is designed on a human scale, with gently curved legs and restrained carving and decoration. Although imposing and architectural in feeling, furniture of this period is not overwhelming. Certain decorative motifs sprang up during the Régence period; they were based on Oriental motifs which emerged full-blown and grotesque in Louis XV, the succeeding style.

To clarify some of the stylistic terms, let's see where they came from and what they meant. The word, *baroque* is a corruption of the Spanish *barrueco*, which means a large, irregularly shaped pearl. The word was for a time confined to the jeweler's craft. It came to denote the extravagant fashions common in the first half of the seventeenth century, chiefly in Italy and France, in which everything was fantastic, florid, and lacking in restraint. The succeeding style, called *rococo* or Louis XV, is also a corruption of two French words drawn from nature: it is a contraction of *rocaille* and *coquille*, loosely translated as rock and shell work, a reference to two popular motifs used for decoration in the Louis XV style. Straight lines and symmetrically balanced arrangements rarely occur in wall paneling, furniture, or other decoration of the period.

The natural reaction to French rococo style occurred during the reign of Louis XVI, where straight lines again predominated over rococo curves. Although Louis XVI style marked a return to classical symmetry, furniture design remained small-scaled, feminine, and formal.

Court style gradually filtered down to the provinces, first to the homes of the country nobility and finally to the public at large. The majority of people living in the countryside was hardly aware of what went on inside a palace or how it was furnished. At each stage of its development, the formal style underwent changes. It was dependent upon the wealth of the owner, the skill of the local craftsmen, the availability of materials, and the differences in regional taste. The people responded most readily to the curves of Louis XV, but local craftsmen greatly modified the curlicues and retained only a gently curved silhouette. The furniture style which evolved, called Country French or French Provincial, includes wardrobes, cabinets, buffets, cupboards, and chairs. French Provincial furniture can still be seen in many parts of France today and is widely reproduced in America and in France. It corresponds in flavor to American Colonial furniture and mixes very well with the latter.

THE METROPOLITAN MUSEUM OF ART

BAROQUE ARMOIRE, *left*, c. 1642–1732, is attributed to one of the leading *ebénistes* of the time, Andre-Charles Boulle. The ornate inlay work of the cabinet, in tortoise shell and exotic woods such as macassar and gabun. in addition to the ormolu mounts, shows the height of French court styling of the Louis XIV period.

Louis XV dressing table, *lower right*, dates from the middle of the eighteenth century. The background woods of mahogany and kingwood are inset with rich marquetry in the form of stylized flowers. The cabriole legs end in scroll feet, adorned with ormolu.

Provincial hutch-cupboard, *far right*, illustrates how the less sophisticated cabinetmakers of the provinces interpreted the formal court styles. This country version of Louis XV design is a masterpiece of proportion and balance. The rococo curves are contained within the straight lines of the door panels and overall outline.

Louis XV console table, *far right*, exemplifies the taste for rococo carving and asymmetrical curves of the period. The carved motifs are loosely based on natural forms such as flowers and shells.

Louis XVI cabinet, *near right*, was made in the last quarter of the eighteenth century and is attributed to another fine *ebéniste*, Adam Weisweiler. The transition from florid curves to severe angularity is seen in this piece. Instead of inlay work or ornate carving, ormolu decoration outlines the top and base and also the three front panels.

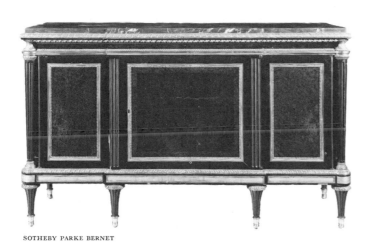

SOTHEBY PARKE BERNET

DON RUSEAU, INC.

SOTHEBY PARKE BERNET

DON RUSEAU, INC.

THE METROPOLITAN MUSEUM OF ART

BAROQUE ARMCHAIR of the Louis XIV period, *left,* is masculine in scale and square in outline. The velvet upholstery is edged in fringe. Square legs, linked by x-shaped stretcher, are gilded.

An armchair of the succeeding period, Louis XV, *top right,* has curved cabriole legs and is delicate and feminine in scale. Such armchairs are called *bergères* because the upholstery wraps around the back and extends beneath the arms.

The armchair, *far right,* has an ornately carved frame in the rococo style and is typical of furniture made for the French court of Louis XV. It is attributed to *ébeniste,* Nicolas Quinibert Foliot, c. 1749.

A gilded side chair of the Louis XVI period, *bottom right,* illustrates the return to straight lines and use of classical motifs in the carving of the frame. It is signed, A. P. Dupain.

This small settee is called a *canape.* Such seating pieces became popular in the late eighteenth century. The straight legs are typically Louis XVI.

DON RUSEAU, INC.

THE METROPOLITAN MUSEUM OF ART

SOTHEBY PARKE BERNET

DON RUSEAU, INC.

EIGHTEENTH-CENTURY ENGLISH STYLES

The eighteenth century is considered the great age of furniture-making, both in England and in France. Design reached a degree of excellence that, connoisseurs of fine antiques believe, has never been equaled. This century dawned with the graceful Queen Anne style (1702–1714) and reached its maturity and waned with the elegant Georgian styles that have become better known by the names of its cabinetmakers: Thomas Chippendale (1718–1779); Thomas Sheraton (1751–1806); and George Hepplewhite (1770–1786).

The eighteenth century was marked by such a flurry in furniture design primarily because of sweeping social changes. Worldwide trade was flourishing. Ships returned from the Orient with spices, tea, and treasures (e.g., china) never before seen by Europeans. Oriental patterns and motifs soon found their way into European designs. Trade fostered new markets, new merchants, and new money. A greater number of people could now afford bigger homes, better furniture; in short, the standard of living was on the rise. Houses were evolving from medieval fortresses and castles into open, airy country houses with large windows, galleries, and gardens.

Along with the increased prosperity and the changing design of houses, furniture was evolving from heavy, rigid, blocklike forms into objects of great refinement and beauty. The paneled styles typical of Elizabethan and Jacobean designs of the seventeenth century were being replaced by furniture more suited to houses than to medieval halls. The first move toward lighter, more livable, and graceful furniture occurred during the reign of William and Mary (1689–1702); the furniture of this period is consequently named after these monarchs. When he ascended the English throne (a result of his marriage to Mary, the English queen) William of Orange brought with him from his native Holland Dutch tastes in furniture and Dutch craftsmen. These motifs soon became anglicized. A taste for curves replaced straight-lined chairs and chests. Dutch veneering, such as marquetry and parquetry, became popular in England, and walnut displaced oak as the predominant wood. By the time of the reign of Queen Anne (1702–1714), furniture had come to resemble the styles with which we are familiar today.

The changes in domestic architecture and the increase in leisure time during Queen Anne's reign led to the creation of all sorts of new items of furniture. The rage for tea drinking called for new serving pieces, such as tea tables, drop-leaf tables, and chests (e.g., lowboys). The acquisition of "china ware" prompted the construction of large, open-fronted cabinets to display it. Entertaining gave rise to game tables and improved sideboards. Comfortable upholstered seating was now a necessity rather than a luxury. Settees and wing-back chairs, as well as armless chairs with specially designed flaring seats to accommodate women's billowing skirts, became commonplace.

Queen Anne furniture possesses an easy charm that is still appreciated today. Its most distinctive feature is the cabriole leg, a delightfully curved leg that is a simplification of an Oriental design. It is found on tables, chairs, as well as on highboy chests, and is often embellished with a scallop shell at the knee or on the apron. Otherwise, decoration is restrained and is usually subservient to the beauty of the wood grain, which is most often walnut. This period is also referred to as "The Age of Walnut."

By the mid-eighteenth century, we have arrived at the age of the great English cabinetmakers—Chippendale, Hepplewhite, and Sheraton. Designers in their own right, the names of these three men have come down to us for yet another reason. Each compiled and published "pattern books" of their designs and all others in vogue at the time. These books were eagerly sought after and the designs were copied by craftsmen in both England and America. As a result, excellent examples of "Chippendale," "Hepplewhite," and "Sheraton" furniture exist which were never seen, much less made, by these cabinetmakers. Their names, however, are linked to a style of furniture which bears certain recognizable design characteristics.

Chippendale furniture actually represents a flowering of the restrained Queen Anne style. (It is also referred to as Georgian furniture, a name derived from the English monarchs, viz. George I, George II, and George III, 1714–1820 inclusive, who reigned at that time. The forms that Chippendale employed remained the same; the tables, chests, cabinets, highboys, wing chairs, and settees all continued to be produced. What did change was the silhouette of the furniture, from the graceful Queen Anne lines to the more robust and masculine lines of Chippendale designs. Carved decoration became more florid and pronounced. The simple pad foot on the Queen Anne cabriole leg evolved into the animal claw clasping a ball, known as the claw-and-ball foot. The gentle fiddleback splat evolved into the intricately carved and pierced Chippendale back splat. During the later phase of his career, Chippendale borrowed heavily from Oriental design motifs; furniture of this period is therefore called "Chinese Chippendale." The cabriole leg disappeared altogether, and was subsequently replaced by a straight, square "Marlborough" leg or by the bracket foot. Fretwork, tracery, fluting, and other decorative elements all appeared in the mid-Georgian period. Mahogany replaced walnut as the preferred material for furniture. Consequently, this period is also called "The Age of Mahogany." Chippendale expanded the range of furniture designs; large architectural bookcases, breakfronts, and desks appeared.

If Chippendale furniture is heavy and robust, Sheraton and Hepplewhite furniture is light and delicate. The latter are somewhat smaller and distinguished by narrow, tapering legs. Hepplewhite furniture uses serpentine fronts with concave or cut-in corners. Chairs with graceful shield, heart, and oval-shaped backs are this designer's most famous creation. Hepplewhite is credited with popularizing the use of satinwood, as well as with using painted decoration on his furniture. Hence, the period is also called "The Age of Satinwood."

The furniture of Thomas Sheraton, although similar to Hepplewhite's in delicacy, is recognizably different from it. Sheraton was actually not a cabinetmaker and no furniture is credited to his manufacture. Sheraton-style furniture has a characteristic rounded and tapered leg that ends in a pointed foot. Chair backs were rectangular

A Manhattan dining room is furnished in typical eighteenth-century English design. Designer David Laurence Roth designed the room around the ceiling decorated in the Adam style with Queen Anne chairs, Savonnerie-style carpet, and Hepplewhite breakfront.
PHOTO: NORMAN MCGRATH

more often than curved, although oval backs were also produced. Sheraton frankly adopted French Louis XVI designs then in vogue on the continent.

In the latter half of the eighteenth century, designers and architects both in France and England were deeply influenced by the discoveries of the ruins of Pompeii and Herculaneum. The decorations of ancient Greece and Rome which were unearthed in the archeological digs inspired and ultimately initiated a classical revival in both architecture and furniture design. The Adam brothers, Robert (1728–1792) and James (1730–1794), English architects who designed splendid palaces for the nobility as well as smaller houses for the middle classes —and designed everything that went into them, too, from furniture to door knobs—did much to spread the vogue for classical decorations. Classical ornaments, such as mythological figures, hexagons, circles, wreaths, medallions, urns, and swags, appeared on furniture and as architectural decoration in interiors. The Adam brothers commissioned Chippendale, Hepplewhite, and other cabinetmakers to produce the furniture for their houses. Today, it is difficult to say who was the original designer of much of this late eighteenth-century furniture.

After the turn of the century, furniture design declined. The English Regency period (1811–1820) saw a rash of decorative revivals and fads that continued into Victorian times. Novelty and oddity held sway; consequently, much of the furniture is less refined and more vulgar than the designs of the previous century. One can find highly amusing pieces from both the Regency and Victorian periods—*faux bambou* cabinets, exotic rattan tables and chairs. Occasional tables, in particular, are delightfully unusual, possessing bases adorned with dolphins, swans, eagles, or dragons.

A remodeled kitchen in Manhattan is furnished with country furniture, English eighteenth-century chairs and a Welsh dresser displaying china.
PHOTO: NORMAN MCGRATH

STAIR & COMPANY

STAIR & COMPANY

STAIR & COMPANY

SOTHEBY PARKE BERNET

DESK AND FOOTSTOOL, *top left,* are classics of Georgian design. Burl veneers on the drawer fronts of the drop-lid desk enhance the simple outline. In typical Georgian fashion, the drawers are shallow at the top and become progressively deeper. Other features are the bracket feet and characteristic brass hardware. The square footstool has cabriole legs decorated with carving on the knees and claw-and-ball feet.

A Hepplewhite sideboard is distinguished by its delicate scale, fine inlay work on the front panels and tapered legs which end in arrowhead feet. The top section of cabinets is gently bowed.

A Queen Anne bureau with bookcase exhibits the best features of the style: the bonnet top accented by three finials, the ball feet, and the teardrop drawer pulls.

The console table, *far left,* with drop leaves and shallow front drawers is a symphony of exotic woods characteristic of the Regency period.

A tallboy, *top right,* also features rich inlay work to animate the chest's stark outlines. The cornice and each of the drawers is banded in feathered veneers of contrasting woods. The chest also has bracket feet and hardware typical of the period.

The Carlton desk, *bottom right,* combines a desk surface with a top section of drawers and compartments. The top is edged with a brass gallery. The first design of this type was reportedly made for Carlton House, the residence of the Prince Regent of England in the eighteenth century.

STAIR & COMPANY

STAIR & COMPANY

31

GEORGIAN MAHOGANY armchair, c. 1750, is distinguished by its bold outlines. Particularly fine are the tracery of the back splat, scalloped seat edge, cabriole legs ending in claw-and-ball feet. All of these features are characteristic of Thomas Chippendale's work.

Hepplewhite armchair, c. 1790, *center,* has a beautifully formed back in the shape of a shield. The reeded legs end in spade feet. The entire frame is decorated with classical motifs and was painted and gilt.

Chippendale armchair, *far right,* has design details illustrating his later work, which was strongly influenced by Chinese motifs. The top rail is shaped like the upturned ends of a pagoda and the back splat features open latticework. The legs are carved to resemble clustered columns.

A Hepplewhite settee, c. 1785, *bottom,* is hand painted with an exotic design of peacock feathers on each shield of the back. The unusual motif is also repeated on the four front legs, which show the early use of casters.

Adam armchair, *far right,* is a particularly fine example of the furniture commissioned by the Adams brothers, architects, for the houses they designed. The frame was carved in classical motifs typical of the period and then was covered with gold leaf. The seat and back are upholstered in the original Gobelin tapestry.

THE METROPOLITAN MUSEUM OF ART

THE METROPOLITAN MUSEUM OF ART

THE METROPOLITAN MUSEUM OF ART

THE METROPOLITAN MUSEUM OF ART

THE METROPOLITAN MUSEUM OF ART

AMERICAN STYLES: COLONIAL TO FEDERAL

The furniture we call Early American or Colonial, produced up to the time of the American Revolution, is rustic and functional, reflecting the era in which it was made and used. Until the beginning of the seventeenth century, life was difficult for the settlers, whose overriding concerns were providing food, shelter, and a safe existence for their families.

At first, furniture was made from the colonists' memory of styles they knew from their native countries. American design followed medieval English design closely, yet it reflected a certain regional variety. Decoration was limited to shallow carving and simple turnings on the legs and stretchers of chairs and tables. Ethnic variety was also a feature of American design; the Pennsylvania Dutch, for instance, decorated their furniture with fine hand-painted folk art. Furniture of the Shakers, on the other hand, was so severely devoid of decoration that it could be mistaken for twentieth-century modern design. More often, colonial furniture resembled its European cottage-furniture ancestors, interpreted with a distinctly American flavor. Typical pieces of the time were Windsor, ladderback, and banister-back chairs; trestle, drop-leaf, and gate-leg tables; and simple chests. The wood used was primarily pine, although the choice often depended upon whatever was locally available—oak, birch, maple, or such fruitwoods as apple or cherry. Because houses of the time were small, furniture that saved space was favored by the anonymous craftsmen. For example, tables with tops that tilted to reveal a seat and folding tables were devised for use in the combination kitchen-living rooms of the time.

Though life for the colonists was hard, ideals ran high. Their practical, rustic furniture was fashioned with much care and skill by American craftsmen. Always popular among collectors, American Colonial furniture is greatly prized today and is widely reproduced.

By the mid-eighteenth century, the colonies prospered, developed commerce, and became self-sufficient. Americans subsequently became style conscious. Houses grew larger and more grand—but never to the same extent as their European counterparts. Furniture was too bulky to import (although some of it was shipped over from England). Skilled craftsmen had emigrated to the New World, where they were busily copying European models or making furniture based on the European pattern books. Furniture centers were established and individual cabinetmakers acquired reputations for the fine quality of their furniture: Samuel McIntire of Salem, Massachusetts; John Goddard and John Townsend of Newport, Rhode Island; William Savery; and Benjamin Randolph of Philadelphia, Pennsylvania. The more beautifully figured walnut gradually replaced the blander pine for sophisticated furniture. Cabinetmakers copied all of the popular English styles, including Chippendale, Hepplewhite, and Sheraton, although the trained eye can distinguish between an American and a European piece. Anyone who has examined a Newport block-front desk by Goddard, with its distinctive reverse-shell motif over each of the three front panels, will not fail to recognize it again. Likewise, the triumph of proportion, scale, and form of a Savery highboy marks it as a true classic of American design.

After the Revolution, America turned to classicism for its design inspiration. Both France and England were experiencing a vogue for classicism, as is evidenced by the work of the Adam brothers in England and the Louis XVI Directoire style in France. The young American nation sympathized with the French struggle for democracy. An amalgamation of the ideals of ancient Greece and Rome, the cornerstone of the classic revival, resulted in the American Federal style. Between 1790 and 1810, some of the finest examples of Federal or post-Colonial furniture and architecture appeared. In the domain of cabinetmaking, Duncan Phyfe, a New Yorker, is justly famous for his superb furniture patterned after Sheraton and the French Directoire style.

Regardless of the sources of its inspiration, American design always remained unique and distinct from its European counterparts. The pieces are more provincial and less sophisticated, show a marked vitality on the part of the artisan, often use less precious woods, carving, or inlay work, yet exude a robust integrity. American folk art—store signs, primitive paintings, early advertising art, quilts, and textiles—as well as the furniture of this period express a tremendous vigor and vitality, American ideals which are prized by collectors and museums alike.

By the nineteenth century, American design, like that of Europe, had degenerated into effusive decoration, overblown proportions, and faddishness. A slight smattering of such later styles as American Empire and Victorian can lend an amusing touch to a decorative scheme. But they should be used sparingly, as an accent, because a roomful of these styles is generally overpowering.

A dining room at the Henry Francis duPont Winterthur Museum enjoys an authentic Colonial ambiance with tavern tables and Windsor chairs (one chair, beneath the hanging cupboard, is Queen Anne in style).
PHOTO: COURTESY OF WINTERTHUR MUSEUM

THE METROPOLITAN MUSEUM OF ART

THE WILLIAM AND MARY highboy, *left*, made in New England about 1700, exemplifies the strength and masterful proportions of early American cabinetry. Each of the eight drawers is surfaced in walnut veneer, outlined with herringbone borders, and decorated with diamond-shaped escutcheons.

A mahogany Chippendale highboy, c. 1750–1780, *top right*, has design features characteristic of William Savery of Philadelphia. The flawless details include the scrolled pediment terminating in rosettes, the intricate tracery of the center panel and central finial, and the robust shell carving of the lower section.

A mahogany block-front kneehole dressing table, *below right*, has carved shells in both concave and convex outlines topping each of the three front panels. These Chippendale details typify the work of cabinet-makers of Newport, Rhode Island, c. 1750–1775, and especially that of the Townsend family.

A provincial slant-top desk of cypress and walnut, *top right*, illustrates how local carpenters interpreted Hepplewhite design details. It was made in Kerr County, Texas, in 1858 by Edward Steves.

The dower chest is beautifully hand-painted to simulate wood graining. Made in the vicinity of Pennsburg, Pa., the chest is inscribed with the owner's name, M. Kriebel, and also with the date of its manufacture.

A tilt-top piecrust table, c. 1750–1780, *bottom right*, has a table top surfaced in highly-figured walnut veneer and finely scalloped edges.

THE METROPOLITAN MUSEUM OF ART

THE SAN ANTONIO MUSEUM ASSOCIATION

THE WHITNEY MUSEUM OF ART

THE METROPOLITAN
MUSEUM OF ART

HISTORIC CHARLESTON PRESERVATION, INC.

THE NEW-YORK HISTORICAL SOCIETY

THE MAHOGANY QUEEN ANNE side chair, *left,* c. 1750, has particularly fine features of the period: the balloon-shaped seat and the cabriole legs, embellished with shell carving on the knees, and ending in claw-and-ball feet. The back splat is carved in the shape of a stylized urn.

The American Empire armchair, *near right,* is attributed to the workshop of Duncan Phyfe of New York, c. 1816. The mahogany frame is decorated with gilt appliqués, such as the acanthus leaf swags on the legs and shoulders of the chair back. The seat and back are covered in a Gobelin tapestry.

A Pilgrim chair, *center,* c. 1650–1700, was made in New England out of native maple and ash wood and was painted black. It is devoid of decoration save the turned spindles of the back and legs and yet it has a strength and purposefulness.

A Colonial corner chair, *far right,* has a typical rush seat and turned legs ending in a duck or Spanish foot. The frame of cherry and ash characteristically was painted black. It was made in New England, possibly Portsmouth, New Hampshire, between 1710 and 1730.

A Windsor settee rocker, *bottom,* was probably made in Pennsylvania, c. 1800–1810. It is distinguished by its fine proportions, the regularity of the turned spindles, and the baby guard rail at one side of the seat. The bench, sometimes called a Deacon's bench, was originally painted dark brown with yellow stripes and a floral decoration.

THE METROPOLITAN MUSEUM OF ART

THE HENRY FRANCIS DU PONT WINTERTHUR MUSEUM

THE NEW-YORK HISTORICAL SOCIETY

THE NEW-YORK HISTORICAL SOCIETY

MODERN: THE STYLE OF OUR TIMES

The style of our times is truly international. It reflects the advances achieved since the eighteenth century, when furniture was painstakingly made by hand, and the nineteenth century, when machines took over the task, to the twentieth century, where new materials and technology have altered our production methods—and our whole way of life. This style successfully utilizes the newer materials (especially metals and synthetics). More important, it questions what an object is, what it does, and what it should look like in an age where men have traveled to the moon.

How did design concepts arrive at this stage? As we have noted, the excellence of design during the eighteenth century was followed by a deterioration of design in the nineteenth century. The Industrial Revolution was fought not on the fields but in factories, not with weapons but with machines. It buried the skill of the craftsman beneath a heap of cheap, machine-made furniture. Because of a burgeoning population and an expanding market, the emphasis in design shifted from making a thing beautiful to making it quickly and cheaply. Mass production, which made possible the creation of a single, uniform product in unlimited quantities, remained untroubled by esthetics.

By the turn of the century, furniture was being made in every conceivable style, with one revival following upon the heels of another. A re-creation of eighteenth century art and decoration, called Beaux Arts, was considered the most appropriate architectural style of the times. The deluge of eclecticism worried sensitive artists and architects. By the 1880s, a revolt to counter the excesses of the machine, called the Arts and Crafts Movement, was started in England by the architect-artist-poet William Morris. It attempted to return to the medieval ideal of the handcraftsman or artisan. Looking backward rather than forward, it ignored the machine's potential. In the 1890s, the movement spawned a stylistic vogue for whiplash curves and naturalistic, vinelike forms, called Art Nouveau. The work of Belgian architect Henri Van de Velde is representative of this style.

Meanwhile, industry was solving design problems without the aid of artists, architects, or designers. In 1840, the Viennese manufacturer Thonet devised a process for producing a simple, lightweight, inexpensive chair by bending beechwood through the application of heat and steam. The bentwood "café" chair, produced in great numbers (seven million had been manufactured by 1891) was right on target for its time.

New principles and new materials lead to the creation of new stylistic forms. A design movement is an outgrowth of the changing social, economic, and technological climate of a given period in time; if it is to have a lasting effect, it must epitomize this moment. Otherwise, a fad will result, like a plant placed in shallow soil which withers at the first hint of harsh conditions. The bentwood café chair had solid roots: honest materials and honest construction. A great design or style in any age derives its esthetic basis from the methods and mores unique to it.

40

In 1907, Henri Van de Velde started a school in Weimar, Germany, called the Deutsche Werkbund. It later moved to Dessau, where it was in operation from 1919 to 1933. The school took a new direction under Walter Gropius and was reorganized as the Bauhaus. The Bauhaus profoundly influenced modern design and reconciled the conflicting aims of art and industry. The school stressed an interdisciplinary education. Every student was trained by two teachers, an artist and a craftsman. The mingling of fine and applied arts, geared to machine capabilities, resulted in "functional" design. In 1925, the architect Marcel Breuer, a faculty member, produced a chair consisting of tubular steel that is considered a classic today. The strength of the steel allowed for a cantilevered seat rising from the upturned base, thus eliminating the back legs; moreover, the chair had a built-in resilience without the aid of springs.

Elsewhere, Finnish architect Alvar Aalto was exploring another material, plywood, composed of a lamination of thin crosslayers of wood. He designed tables, chairs, and chaise longues constructed of plywood. These designs, too, had superior strength and resilience. Le Corbusier, a French architect (his real name was Charles Édouard Jeanneret; he preferred the French word meaning "the crow"), designed elegantly simple tubular steel-and-leather chairs and a chaise longue produced by Thonet in the late 1920s. Architect Mies van der Rohe capped the achievement for machine elegance with his steel-and-leather, x-based armless chair with a cantilevered seat, which he designed for the German Pavilion at the Barcelona International Exhibition of 1929; ever since, his creation has been known as the "Barcelona chair." From then on, "form follows function" was the underlying credo of all good design.

Political circumstances in Germany during the 1930s led to the disbandment of the Bauhaus. Its members scattered across Europe; several, including Gropius, Breuer, and Josef Albers, came to America. But the school's influence was hardly felt outside of art and design circles.

More popular and better known was Art Deco, a modernistic style which derived its name from the Exposition Internationale des Arts Décoratifs held in Paris in 1925. Art Deco (the decorative arts counterpart of Art Moderne, a term which was more frequently applied to architecture, although the terms are often used interchangeably) is characterized by a vaguely geometric, Egyptian-influenced angularity. Like Art Nouveau, Art Deco was unconcerned with economic and social conditions. In retrospect, it may be viewed as a transitional movement, moving away from excessive decoration toward a sense of streamlined modernity.

Throughout this period, Scandinavian design retained its strong craft tradition. It employed the machine as a teamworker and helper of the artisan, easing his job without compromising design integrity. Scandinavian designs, such as the chairs and tables of the Swede Bruno Mathsson, the Finn Alvar Aalto, and the Danes Finn Juhl and Hans Wegner, rank as artistry in wood.

America contributed very little to the stylistic innovations of the 1920s and 1930s. In 1941, however, Eero Saarinen (son of Finnish architect Gottlieb Eliel Saarinen) and Charles Eames won a Museum

of Modern Art competition for functional furniture that marked a design breakthrough: a chair of molded plywood shells for seat and back fitted with foam rubber upholstery; and a dining group of tables and chairs mounted on pedestals rather than legs. Since the Bauhaus, furniture had been "losing" its legs: two was better than four; now one seemed best of all. Eames went on to design another classic in 1956, the leather-and-rosewood lounge chair.

In the 1960s, Italy emerged as the center of innovative furniture design. Once again, social changes and technology provided the springboard for new design. Plastic, in particular, gained a reputation as a viable furniture material, not simply as a wood substitute, but as a material in its own right. Designers found the expressive force of these newer materials: plastic molded well and assumed rounded, amorphic shapes; urethane foam lent itself to interesting upholstery forms. Rigid and severe straight lines gave way to softer, voluptuous curves. The hard edge of the 1950s was replaced by the soft edge of the 1970s.

So where are we today? Space is contracting in the average living environment. Ceilings have dropped nearly six feet since the turn of the century. Square footage per capita continues to shrink; spaces meant to be inhabited by one or two persons are being lived in by four. Space has become a true luxury. Modular furniture composed of components provides for more flexible furniture arrangements within a given space. Manufacturers can shorten their line and still meet the public's needs. Instead of purchasing two-, three-, and four-seat sofas, the customer can buy what he needs from a modular group and put them together himself. No longer are separate pieces of furniture the answer. A sofa and end tables can be designed to form one unit. The back of the seating unit can have storage cabinets or bookshelves. Removing the clutter of individual pieces of furniture makes the space look and live better. This visual freedom, coupled with the sumptuous curves and inviting shapes of today's upholstered furniture, have removed the stigma of sterility from the modern living environment.

A suburban home was remodeled by Joseph D'Urso as a background for contemporary furnishings, including the bentwood chairs, parson's dining table, and two white ashwood lounge chairs designed by Alvar Aalto. Banquettes provide soft seating.
PHOTO: RICHARD CHAMPION

A DINING CHAIR of Reglar, a fiberglass reinforced polyester, is called the Gaudí chair and was designed by Vico Magestretti in 1967. It and the accompanying table, called the Stadio 80, typify the growing sophistication and elegance of molded plastic furniture. Both are manufactured by Artemide of Milan.

This pedestal dining table, with laminated top and cast plastic base, was considered revolutionary when Eero Saarinen designed it in 1956.

A portable bar cart with oversized wheels looks like a playful design of the 1970s yet it was designed by Finnish architect Alvar Aalto in 1936. The frame is made of steam bent birch and the top surfaces are laminated in linoleum. It is manufactured by Artek of Finland.

Stacking shelves and cabinets are made of ABS plastic and were designed by Anna Castelli Ferrieri in 1970. They illustrate the trend toward stacking storage units and modular components to replace one-piece chests. The units are manufactured by Kartell of Milan.

CASTELLI FURNITURE INC.

KNOLL INTERNATIONAL

44

ICF INTERNATIONAL

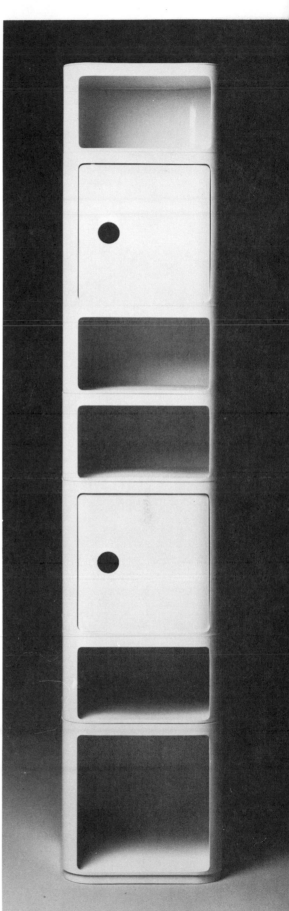

BEYLERIAN, LTD.

R & G AFFILIATES

THE MUSEUM OF MODERN ART

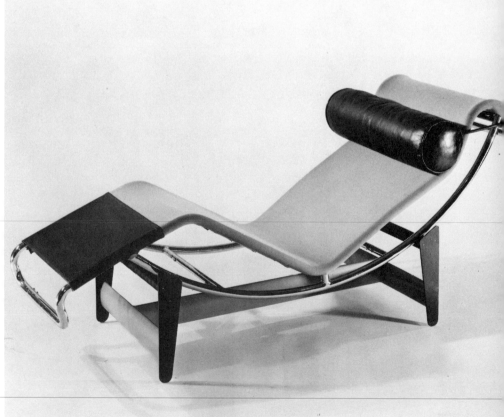

THE MUSEUM OF MODERN ART

THE MUSEUM OF MODERN ART

CASTELLI FURNITURE INC.

MODERN DESIGN CLASSICS, *left page, clockwise:* The Cesca chair was designed by Marcel Breuer in 1928 and was first produced by Thonet, a firm that has been associated with the growth of contemporary furniture since the early nineteenth century. At the time, Breuer's use of tubular steel for the cantilevered frame, which holds the cane seat and back, was considered revolutionary.

This lounge chair and ottoman was designed by Charles Eames in 1956. The shell is molded rosewood plywood and the cushions are covered in leather. It is manufactured by Herman Miller of Zeeland, Michigan.

An adjustable chaise longue designed in 1927 by Le Corbusier, in collaboration with Pierre Jeanneret and Charlotte Perriand, has a chrome-plated tubular-steel frame that is wrapped in a leather sling. It was first produced by Thonet.

The Barcelona chair, a masterpiece of twentieth century elegance, was designed by Mies van der Rohe in 1929 for the German exposition at Barcelona in the same year.

Two early bentwood chairs, *near left,* are examples of the mass-produced designs introduced by Thonet between 1860 and 1876. The armless Vienna café chair has been a record-breaking best seller since its introduction in the 1850s.

The folding chair, *top right,* designed by Gian Carlo Peretti in 1969 and manufactured by Castelli of Milan, shows the ingenuity of modern designers at reinterpreting an accepted design in new materials.

The stacking chair, *lower right,* designed by Joe Colombo in 1967, was an early and highly successful attempt at molding plastic into furniture designs. It is manufactured by Kartell of Milan.

R & G AFFILIATES

R & G AFFILIATES

BEYLERIAN, LTD.

SPACE PLANNING

The last status symbol of the twentieth century is space.

John Saladino

BEAUTIFUL ROOMS REPRESENT a perfect balance between the physical space and the elements that go into it. Space and objects must achieve a sense of equilibrium. When one tends to dominate the other, either the room looks cold, unfurnished, and antiseptic or it appears crowded and stuffed. The quality of the space itself is no longer perceived; the room becomes a container full of things.

The goal of interior design is to assemble all the elements—the furnishings, materials, colors, lighting—so that they form an imaginative and attractive composition. But interiors are judged not only in terms of appearance but also with respect to function. The proper division of space, its allocation in the most effective and functional way, involves determining the traffic flow, planning for activities, and affirming the relationship of scale and mass both to the space and to each other. It's impossible and foolish to leave such complicated space planning to mere guesswork. We need something tangible to work with in translating our ideas into a finished decorative scheme. In short, we need a plan.

The floor plan is a two-dimensional sketch of a three-dimensional space. It is the map upon which to chart the passageways of the house, to determine the traffic flow; it is a diagram of spatial geometry which reveals the best possibilities for allocating centers of activity. It locates the living areas—the best place to sit, to entertain, to hide a study, to find a quiet reading corner, to place the TV, or to situate peripheral activities that might not have an obvious place of their own.

Practically speaking, it is nearly impossible to proceed with a decorating project without a floor plan. Knowing the length of the wall where the sofa will be placed tells us how long the sofa ought to be, what size rug to place in the room, how many chairs it can hold, what sort of storage cabinetry we need. Without this data, we run the real risk of either filling up the room so that no one can walk through it with ease or buying furniture that simply doesn't fit.

Remembering the rule that "form follows function," the furniture will logically fall into place on the floor plan. A checklist of the family's activities provides a work summary, or program of information, to determine what sort of furniture is needed and where it is to be placed. Certain needs are nearly universal regardless of family size—seating, storage, dining—but the amount of space dictates how those needs are to be met. The home of a large suburban family with a young Toscanini who practices daily at the Steinway grand piano will certainly

Designer Ward Bennett's apartment in the Dakota is a tour de force of modern design. The only furnishings are those which are essential.
PHOTO: RICHARD CHAMPION

The converted loft of art dealer Ivan
Karp presents the perfect equilibrium
between American folk art objects
and modern furnishings, within the
envelope of the modern architecture.
PHOTO: MICHAEL GEIGER

differ from that of a single girl who has to satisfy all her physical and psychological needs in a one-room studio apartment. The floor plan is the organizer. Like a good desk with lots of cubbyholes, it sorts out and files the data and helps bring a sense of unity to the chaotic existence of a family.

By providing a bird's eye view of the space, the floor plan uncovers the possibilities for structural changes. Looking at a room from above and observing the sequence of spaces flowing into or adjoining it may suggest that relocating a doorway or installing a partial divider will add immeasurably to the experience of entering, looking into, or living in a room. The potential for structural changes as small as moving an electrical outlet or as great as ripping out an entire wall become visible on the floor plan.

Drawing Up a Floor Plan

The floor plan is nothing more than a simple sketch of the outlines of the room to be furnished. The length of the four walls should be measured accurately. These dimensions are then transferred to graph paper using a scale of a quarter inch for every foot of actual space. Windows, doorways, and any architectural features—a fireplace, a staircase, supporting columns, or other permanent jogs—are also measured and recorded on the floor plan. This plan, if properly drawn to scale with all of the architectural data in place, will serve as the worksheet for the overall design. Sheets of tracing paper can be placed over the floor plan to try out different furniture arrangements.

Here are several principles to bear in mind when recording the furniture on the floor plan:

Determine the traffic pattern first. Mark the natural line of movement from room to room and throughout the central space. Because traffic flows along these paths, they should be kept free of obstacles. Furniture should not force people to squeeze through the space, nor hamper free passage along any of these lines. (There is an exception to this general rule, however. Sometimes it is advantageous to block off a traffic path either to create an intimate space within a larger area or to gain a greater degree of flexibility in furniture placement—for instance, where walls are broken up by a profusion of windows or doors. Placing the back of a sofa in the middle of a room redirects the flow of traffic around it. The sofa arrests traffic both physically and visually and serves as a partial room divider.)

Determine the zones of activity. The line of movement or traffic pattern will automatically create sectioned off areas, thus dividing the various rooms into zones. These, in turn, become centers of activity. In a living room, the largest zone is often the best place to plan a major conversation grouping of furniture. Smaller zones might be ideal for a reading chair with an ottoman, a desk, or a game table. Odd, leftover spaces which at first glance appear lost in space often turn out to be space bonuses—a spot for a window seat, space for bookshelves or for displaying a collection, or an area for an indoor garden.

Situate the largest pieces of furniture first. This might include a sofa, a piano, an important armoire, or a storage wall. With these in place, the smaller items of furniture will logically fall into place around them; for example, an occasional chair would normally be near the sofa, with necessary tables between them.

Design your interior with the natural light source and view in mind; the way the light falls naturally in the space often dictates how and where furniture should be placed. Most people prefer to sit in the lightest, sunniest part of the room. The major seating group may gravitate toward a bay window possessing a good view. (Remember, though, that nothing is more uncomfortable than facing the glare of bright sunlight. The sofa could be placed at right angles to the window.) In a bedroom, the light might dictate positioning the bed out of the direct path of the light—and away from window drafts. The desk or reading chair would naturally be placed with its back to the light.

Design your interior to create a sense of balance. With the large furniture in place and the auxiliary furniture grouped around it, it becomes obvious if the room is unbalanced. The combined mass of the major seating area requires a complementary mass in another part of the space. Sometimes the architecture itself provides for this—a bank of bay windows or a staircase, for instance—or it can be provided by furniture, such as a secondary seating group, a wall of bookshelves, or a grand piano. Furniture masses should be distributed evenly so that they don't weight one side of the space and leave the other side empty.

Plan a half-and-half mix of upholstered and wood furniture. This is a common decorator's trick and is very effective in keeping the scheme in balance. Upholstered furniture should be separated by alternating wood tables and chests. A half-and-half mix prevents the room from taking on a spindly look; as Billy Baldwin has said, "A room full of chair and table legs looks restless." Upholstery adds softness to the total scheme, while the wood pieces provide an architectural solidity.

Design your interior around a natural focal point. When you enter a room, there is usually one element in particular that catches your eye. The fireplace is always a focal point; so is a good view. Many rooms have one or, at most, two places that suit the positioning of the sofa best, according to Barbara D'Arcy, who spent fourteen years designing model rooms for Bloomingdale's in New York City. The sofa should face the room's best feature, or natural focal point. If the room doesn't have a strong focus or an arresting feature that rivets the eye, then one must be created. This can be accomplished with a tall armoire, an étagère, or, in a modern scheme, with a wall of mirrors, a row of built-in banquettes flanked by bookcases, or a sizable work of art.

Avoid lining up furniture against the sides of the room. The most imaginative furniture arrangements often occur when the furniture is placed in the room's center. Two loveseats facing each other before the fireplace, for instance, is more creative than one long three-seater set against the wall. A central furniture arrangement creates "psychological space." It surrounds the furniture with a free air flow and preserves the room's architectural presence. These schemes often have a quality of lightness or airiness which makes the room appear larger than it is.

Place furniture in logical groupings. Seating areas require adjacent surfaces to hold glasses, ashtrays, magazines, and books. Lounge

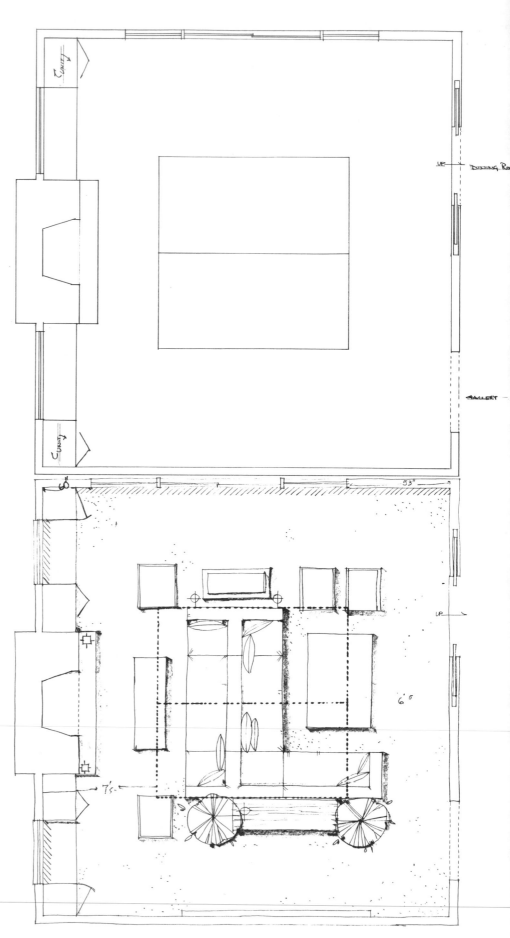

THE FLOOR PLAN of a room, such as the living room shown here, is drawn to show the placement of all the windows, doorways, the fireplace, and other architectural features. The square outline in the center of the space indicates an overhead skylight.

The furniture is then placed in the plan by drawing the outlines of the actual pieces to their exact dimensions. This is usually done in a scale of ¼ inch equals a full foot. Here, designers Robert Patino and Vincent Wolf used two sofas as the nucleus of the scheme, placing them back-to-back in the room's center with the occasional chairs and tables grouped around them. This creates two separate conversation areas, one facing the fireplace and a larger grouping facing the room's entrance. The advantage of such a plan is that it concentrates the seating in the room's center, allows a good traffic pattern around it, and preserves the room's sense of spaciousness.

With the furniture in place, the designers next positioned the room's lighting. The lighting plan, *top right*, shows a series of wall washers along the perimeter of the room, interspersed with downlights and pin spots for accent lighting, such as over a large plant.

A rendering of the living room shows the complete scheme with plants and accessories in place.

PLANS COURTESY OF ROBERT PATINO ASSOCIATES, INC.

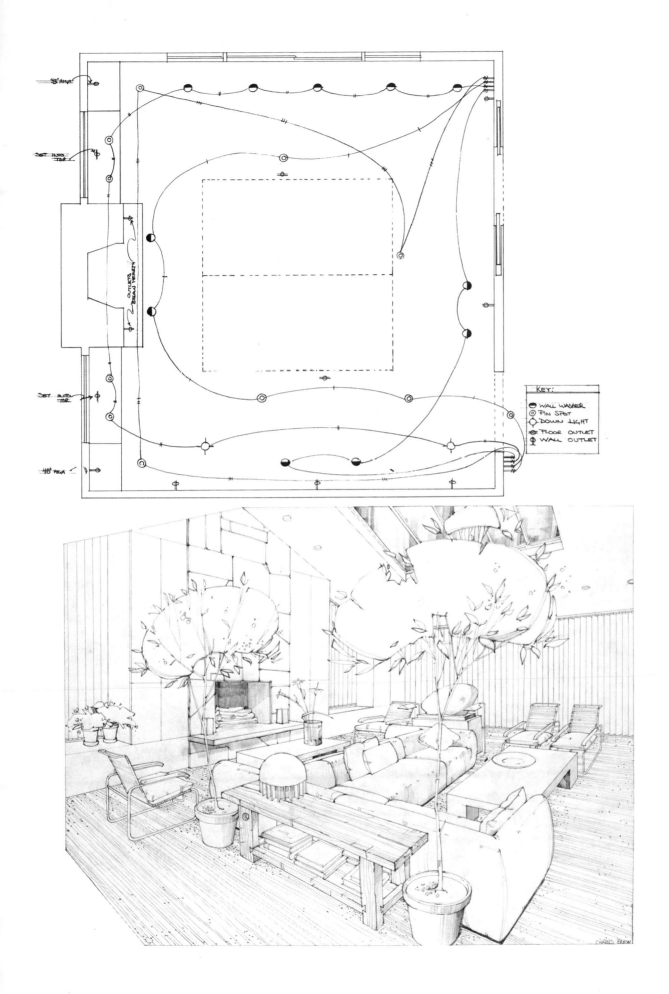

CHARLES BROWN

chairs should have an ottoman and be near a reading light and a table. Divide the furniture into small, separate yet logical groupings so that each unit creates a small, informal area within the larger space. Area rugs, folding screens, bookcases, and étagères are subtle yet effective area definers that do not check the spatial flow.

Alternate between tall and short furniture. Contrasting the vertical and horizontal elements in a room avoids dull or uninteresting juxtapositions and gives the eye a sense of variety. Although the relative weight of a piece of furniture, i.e., its bulk, will show up on the floor plan, it's height or verticality will not. A good rule of thumb to follow is to avoid placing two tall objects side by side without an intervening horizontal element. For instance, if a grandfather clock is placed beside an armoire both vie for the eye's attention. It would be much better to place a loveseat or chair between the two, or perhaps even a lot of blank wall space.

Keep a sense of scale in mind. Scale, like verticality, is difficult to assess on a floor plan. Designers constantly strive to keep furniture in proper scale with the rest of the room. If a room is rather small, they may prefer to use a loveseat rather than a long sofa since the former's smaller size is clearly better suited to the overall dimensions of the room. Tables and most other furnishings would likewise be small in scale because of visual and spatial necessity. On the other hand, a very large room may require two large sofas and a complement of occasional chairs in conversational groupings to give it a well-furnished look. Using furniture of overwhelming size will unavoidably dwarf smaller pieces next to it. Too much regularity in furniture size leads to dullness. It's better to err on the side of large-scale furniture. Small furniture looks insignificant, while an imposing piece can turn out to be a decorative flourish.

Experiment with several schemes. Sometimes a furniture arrangement just naturally falls into place. More often, experimentation and exploration of other possibilities generates a far more lively and original answer. There are literally innumerable ways to furnish a room; the floor-plan stage is the best time to try them all out. Once the scheme has been implemented and the furniture has been purchased and is on its way, the decision is final. It is far better to mull over the floor plan and carry it with you when shopping for furniture. A careful consideration of all the options open to you can set the decorating scheme off in a whole new direction.

Consider modular and built-in furniture. In recent years, furniture has been moving off the floors and onto the walls. Cantilevered shelves, built-in banquettes that also serve as table surfaces, and seating cushions on carpeted platforms are growing in popularity. Eliminating the jumble of chair legs of free-standing furniture opens up the space and lends a sense of spatial freedom to the room. (It is also an invaluable aid in terms of upkeep and maintenance.)

Design your interior for continuity. Think of the house as a whole, not merely as a series of isolated rooms. Sequences of spaces, i.e., how rooms open into other rooms, make an important decorative impact. Textures on floors, wall colors, and various patterns on wallpaper can either create a pleasing continuity throughout the house or a cacophony of unrelated effects which are visually disturbing.

Plan for the future. Rooms need not be completely furnished in one fell swoop. Fill in the bare spots with a large, tree-sized plant, preferably in a planter on casters. A room containing less furniture often turns out to be a limitation which is actually highly flattering to any space. People today are using less rather than more furniture in their decorating schemes to create a free, fluid flow of space.

Fill in areas with lighting. Once the floor plan has been drawn up and the final furniture arrangement decided upon, the lighting scheme can be determined. Plan for a variety of lighting: lamps by the major seating areas; a floor lamp or other suitable reading light by the lounge chairs; suspended lighting over the game table. Designers today prefer to keep the light source hidden whenever possible. They consequently favor track lighting for its versatility; low lights hidden in plants; lights recessed behind shelves or ceiling coves; or sometimes light emanating as a line at the base of cabinets. (The various ways to use light will be discussed in a subsequent chapter.)

Although planning a room on paper is essential, many a decorator admits that even after all the preliminary arrangements have been made, once the furniture arrives on the scene and the various objects are positioned in the physical space, changes still have to be made. Visual and psychological aspects that could not possibly be revealed on paper come into play. And so, too, does the way the room is actually used by its inhabitants. A bookcase will look too cramped in the space intended when viewed from the door and may consequently have to be pulled an inch or two this way or that. Spaces which we originally estimated would be wide enough to pass comfortably by a desk or table suddenly "feel" too tight for easy movement. Furniture will get jostled and pulled about; chairs which were placed at right angles to the sofa will be repositioned at a slant. These shifts and movements do not mean that we have made a mistake. They are the minor adjustments that create a good "fit." Like a couturier who first makes a pattern and then cuts a dress for a client, the first fitting is crucial. Relatively minor adjustments, like lifting the shoulder seam and tucking in the bodice, create a glovelike fit. The same holds true for a furniture floor plan: a pattern has been made to suit the physical dimensions of a room, yet it still requires minor adjustments to satisfy the eye.

FURNITURE WITH STAYING POWER

I could never afford to be fashionable, simply because what is fashionable this year is poison the next. If one can afford to indulge, have fun, throw it out, that's one thing. I've never been able to.

Van Day Truex

IF ARCHITECTURE is the structure, or bare bones, of a space, then furniture is the muscle. It fleshes out the room and makes the empty space habitable. Furniture lends a certain character to a room which determines whether we call it "modern" or "traditional." Stylistic considerations aside, furniture represents a considerable investment. It takes the largest chunk out of most decorating budgets and therefore deserves careful thought and selection. The three primary questions to ask when buying furniture are:

1. What will it be used for?
2. Will it fit?
3. Is it a good value?

Since the question of style has already been discussed in a previous chapter, the only thought that might be added here is a mention of fashion. Furniture, like clothing, is subject to the vagaries of fads, albeit to a more limited degree. Anything that is so overwhelmingly *au courant* that it runs the risk of falling from favor in a short time should be avoided. This is particularly true of fabric and wallpaper designs.

A floor plan is the best guide as to whether or not a given amount of furniture will fit into a room. The homework involved in drawing up a floor plan will indicate whether a room needs a loveseat, three- or four-seat sofa, or several modules of sectional seating. It will indicate how many occasional chairs, tables, storage chests, or bookcases will comfortably fit into a room and where they will be placed. The floor plan also dictates furniture size. If, for instance, the area between two windows measures three feet, then, after allowing for a comfortable distance from each window, the piece selected for that spot, whether it be a desk or a console table, cannot be wider than two feet three inches. The same reasoning holds true for every piece of furniture selected for that particular space.

It would be ideal if we could all begin our decorating plans from scratch. For most of us, that will not be the case. We will have to incorporate into the scheme our old sofa, or rug, or draperies, Grandmother's breakfront, or the dining table and chairs we bought as newlyweds. It complicates the planning but most of the furnishings can be blended into the new decorative plan with success.

In the case of upholstered furniture, slipcovers offer an ideal solution for recycling the couch or chairs. Good upholstery shops and

A bull's eye mirror hanging above the fireplace which is inlaid with antique Delft tiles is a strong focal point for the furniture mix in an apartment designed by John Robert Moore.
PHOTO: TOM WIER

the better department stores all offer both slipcovering and upholstery services. Assess the worth of the piece in question, in terms of your decorative scheme, because slipcovers are not cheap. Good ones (those that fit like a glove) are nearly as costly as reupholstering the piece of furniture. And reupholstering a sofa or chair can cost nearly as much as replacing it with a new one.

On the other hand, some of the older styles of upholstery are so handsome that they will be worth the investment. A well-known New York decorator has recovered his eleven-year-old sofa three times, not because of wear, but because he wished to change the color scheme of his room. And he also has a set of chintz slipcovers for his summertime decorative look. He had purchased an expensive, custom-made sofa to begin with and today couldn't replace it for the same price.

Wood furniture can also be integrated into a new scheme with some ingenuity. The heirlooms we inherited from our parents will not give us trouble in decorating, but those first purchases made as newlyweds probably will. The blond wood dining set, for instance, or that dark wood Mediterranean bedroom suite. To play down the furniture use a bold wall color. For the dining room with the blond furniture, try red, charcoal brown or emerald green, which causes the furniture to become secondary in importance. (A new lighting scheme can also remove the emphasis from the furniture.) For the Mediterranean bedroom set, try a new decorating scheme based on printed fabrics: a new bedspread, draperies, and a new carpet. They may transform the room so that everything seems fresh and new.

If the furniture is not valuable, either in terms of resale or sentimental value, then try something daring. Paint it, stencil it, or use one of the many kits on the market to give it an antique finish. There is nothing to lose with this approach, and the piece of furniture may end up an important adjunct to the new scheme after all.

Re-using carpeting is difficult but not impossible with today's selection of wall-paint colors and fabrics. (Dyeing carpet, however, is not successful and is quite expensive.) But wall-to-wall carpeting, especially if it is patterned and hard to use as it is in the new scheme, can be cut down and the edges bound to make an area rug. Large carpet pieces, such as those from a living room, can be used as stair runners or to carpet smaller rooms. Think creatively about recycling old furnishings—they may turn into a money-saving bonus.

Furniture, regardless of its price, should be practical, easy to maintain, and able to stand up under constant use. This rule applies equally to a fine antique secretary or to an Italian modern chair. Comfort and durability are the prime requirements. The backbone of the living room is the upholstered seating. Sofas that are too soft, without firm back support, or are so deep that they hit the back of the knees are obviously uncomfortable. Dining chairs that look great until one sits down are to be avoided. The most elegant dinner can be ruined by an uncomfortable chair.

It's wise to try out the furniture while it is still on the selling floor —even though the sales person may not take kindly to the idea. Sit in chairs and rock on them; bounce on sofas; go through the motions of rising, settling in, and getting out of lounge chairs. Think of the way the furniture would be used at home. This test often reveals a host of uncomfortable features that may not be visible to the naked eye. Open cabinet doors; look at the backs of drawers and the bottoms of chairs; notice whether the backs of cabinets are constructed of pressed board stapled in place or of wood, whether they are finished or unfinished. If a piece of furniture looks poorly made or feels rickety to begin with, a year's use will probably finish it off.

Proportion, line, balance, and form are all important in choosing furniture—and the hardest concepts to convey in words. What we are after is good design and well-constructed furniture. Only a trained eye and repeated exposure can teach that lesson. Two trips to different stores can provide an instant lesson in quality and good design. It can reveal more about furniture construction and the difference between quality and shoddiness than an entire chapter. Visit the most expensive furniture store in the city; browse through the various departments; examine the furniture; notice the sheen and luster of the wood grain and finish; study the appearance of the piece; sit in the sofas and easy chairs. Spend at least an hour luxuriating in the atmosphere of the furniture. Regardless of how much money has been set aside for furniture in your budget, visit the most expensive antique dealer in town. (Here it will be for purposes of looking rather than touching.) Spend a long time surveying the furniture. Try to determine what makes it beautiful. Is it the strong, robust outlines of the piece? Is it the beautiful finish, the fine wood grain, the carefully matched veneer, the superb carving of the wood decoration, the hardware? Or is it all of these qualities?

Now take a trip to the furniture store selling the flimsiest, lowest-priced wares. Go through the same motions of sitting, settling in, and rising from upholstered seating. Notice the quality of the materials used; look at the backs of cabinets and drawers. The difference between fine versus inferior craftsmanship, between good and bad proportion, between quality and shoddy construction should become glaringly apparent.

If there are good public museums and/or private historic mansions within easy reach, take a trip and inspect their interior furnishings. The purpose of these excursions is to train the eye to recognize and evaluate simple, good proportions; purity of line, balance, and symmetry; fine materials and fine woods—in short, overall appearance. A comparison between the best available furniture and the worst says volumes. Once design and quality have been discerned, good value naturally follows.

Looking for Value

There are two approaches in determining how much and on what one should spend furniture dollars—and both have merit. Some designers stress the importance of purchasing only high-quality furniture that will give years of lasting service. They advocate custom-made furniture, sofas and chairs made to order at special upholstery shops where materials and craftsmanship can be supervised. For wood furniture, such as cabinets and chests, they prefer antiques, wherever possible, rather than reproductions or commercially made furniture. In the minds of many designers, reproductions are not a good investment. They are expensive to begin with and have little, if any, resale value. Because of the rising cost of skilled labor for hand carving and the expense of fine wood, the price of a good reproduction now approaches that of a lesser antique. Reproductions, regardless of how well they are made and how esthetically pleasing they may be, are judged as new furniture.

A number of designers take the opposite approach on the question of buying furniture. They select furniture that suits the purpose at hand and disregard the idea of furniture as an investment. By the time people are ready to move or update their furniture, they will welcome a complete change. Young people, in particular, appreciate this view. The "life" of the furniture we put in our homes is surprisingly long. Recent studies set the average life of a sofa (i.e., how long a family keeps it before replacement) at twenty years; mattresses have a lifespan of eleven years. By that time, our furniture has more than paid for itself, regardless of how much we originally paid for it.

Budgetary considerations will determine whether a given piece of furniture represents the best value for the price. Clearly, someone with unlimited funds will select furniture quite differently from someone who is working within a strict budget. Value is the key word. One must always ask: Is this the best value for the amount being paid?

Value cuts across all stylistic boundaries. Whether a piece is modern or antique, it has a value depending upon one's budget. Four director's chairs at $35 apiece may be the best value for struggling newlyweds, whereas a matched set of four antique Philadelphia Chippendale dining chairs of exceptional rarity and in excellent condition may be a good investment at $5,000 apiece to the executive who just reaped a windfall profit in the stock market.

It is the man or woman in the middle-income area who has the hardest time finding good value and avoiding the trap of decorating clichés. Moderately priced furniture includes a host of mediocre, badly designed pieces that are overpriced for what they offer in the way of materials and construction. The most bastardized pseudostyles of furniture are found in this price category. Avoiding such furniture requires homework and a trained eye. (More on this can be found in the chapter on budget.) The danger in buying cheap furniture is in its poor construction and use of shoddy materials. The pitfall of moderately priced furniture is its stylistic pretention, its claim to be something which it is not. The days of the skilled craftsman who hand carved wood and performed skillful joinery techniques have all but vanished. That sort of craftsmanship, when found on a fine piece of cabinetry, will reflect a comparable quality; the price will also be commensurately high.

Much has been written about wood furniture construction. Books describe such important construction details as mortise-and-tenon joinery and dovetailed drawers. Most of this information has become obsolete, however, since nowadays nearly all furniture in a middle price range is basically made the same way. The cheaper the line, the more shortcuts employed in its construction. Wood will consist of thin veneers rather than solid panels. This is not to say that all veneering is bad. On the contrary, fine detail work, such as parquetry and marquetry or banding of exotic woods, is a sign of exquisite workmanship and is usually found on rare antiques. Plastic, too, is no longer a dirty word in the furniture industry—as long as it does not try to imitate wood. Molded plastic designed to simulate carved wood decoration signals low quality, whereas colorful plastic tables and stackable bookshelves, storage bins, and cubes are tough, durable, and an excellent buy for the money.

It Pays to Shop Around

The floor plan tells us what types of furniture we need and the correct size. Our personal preferences tell us what kind of piece to look for. The next step is finding it. A good value can only be located by comparison shopping. Regardless of the amount of one's decorating budget, canvassing the stores and seeing what is available—and at what price—can be enlightening. In all categories of furniture, from antiques to modern plastic items, prices vary greatly from place to place.

Price alone should not be the sole consideration in determining whether or not to buy a piece of furniture. Perhaps you are considering the purchase of an antique at two different dealers' establishments. Dealer X's Georgian tea table may be considerably less expensive than dealer Y's. Are the tables really comparable? Or is there some other reason for the disparity in price? Has one table been restored or altered? Is one a finer specimen that will fetch more money when the time comes to resell it?

This line of questioning applies to new furniture as well. Markups vary from one department store to another within the same city—frequently for identical lines of furniture. Stores are notoriously secretive about revealing the names of the manufacturers of their furniture. This explains why so few furniture brand names are known to the public. Certain stores demand exclusive rights to a particular line of furniture; their designers work with the manufacturer in developing it especially for that store. More often, however, the manufacturer will grant a store an exclusive line after making minor alterations, such as changing the drawer pulls and hardware or putting a plinth base on a chest that originally had four legs. The price of furniture which is comparable in terms of style and appearance may vary greatly between competing stores.

Be prepared for disappointments. Quality control is one of the furniture industry's major headaches. Nothing is more frustrating than receiving that long-awaited piece of furniture only to find it damaged or scratched. Dealing with a store you trust will make returns and replacements less of an ordeal.

Delivery is another exasperating fact of life. Furniture has a delivery period that varies from three to six weeks after the order is placed; sometimes this period can extend to as long as ten to twelve weeks. There really is no solution to the interminable delays in furniture deliveries—except if one chooses to buy at auction or at manufacturers' closeouts, where selection is usually minimal.

A reputable furniture or department store is not the only safe alternative when buying furniture. The most fashionable designers and decorators are incredibly astute shoppers. They have no qualms about exploring every avenue to search out treasures in unconventional places. Many are addicted to auction houses and frequent the second-hand shops as readily as they do the finest antique dealers. Flea markets and Goodwill Industries yield interesting and offbeat home furnishings. Any place is fair game to find that elusive piece of furniture which is just right for a room.

Here are some pointers to bear in mind when selecting furniture:

Carefully consider the function or purpose of the furniture. A chair for the foyer need not be as comfortable or functional as one intended for the dining room. It can, for instance, be considerably more decorative or have an interesting carved back since it will rarely be used for sitting.

Consider the problem from a creative angle; this will greatly expand your furniture options. For example, a storage unit could consist of a chrome-and-glass étagère, a colorful, modern plastic bookshelf, an antique English secretary, or an Early American cupboard. Each of these would physically fit the space, but which would give the total decorative scheme the most cachet?

Carry a floor plan with you at all times. If a Victorian *faux bambou* armoire turns up at a garage sale or antique show while you are miles from home, it's a snap to tell whether it will fit in the given space.

Keep an open mind for unexpected finds. An amusing piece of furniture or an oddity can be just what an ultra-serious scheme needs. An unusual Victorian fainting couch or a huge brass bed could become a decorative tour de force.

When selecting mass-produced furniture, avoid anything that purports to be what it is not. Plastic decoration intended to look like wood carving, cheap hardware made to simulate gold, and such meaningless stylistic labels as "French Provincial," "Mediterranean," "Italian," are all warning signals.

Think about maintenance. Be wary of furniture with many spokes, ridges, grooves, and galleries that might be dust collectors, unless your budget allows a retinue of servants.

Don't limit your decorative scheme to one style. Good design cuts across stylistic barriers. A mixture of styles gives the scheme variety—and a personal imprint.

Explore the use of industrial products and materials. Industrial products are inherently rugged and functional. Pirelli rubber flooring, metal display racks from stores, hospital carts, boat hardware, and factory lampshades are just some of the products that have found their way into the home. One designer uses a brightly painted orange and stainless steel mechanic's tool chest in his bedroom instead of a conventional chest of drawers. The shallow drawers are ideal for holding cufflinks and the assorted contents of pants pockets overnight. The large bottom tray, originally intended for tools, is just the right size and depth for three stacks of laundered shirts. It's mounted on oversized casters to make vacuuming the area under it a breeze.

Don't compromise. Wait until the right piece comes along instead of loading the house with substitutes. Furniture is replaced slowly. We end up living with our mistakes for years to come.

Don't overspend and overbuy. We need far less furniture than we think. An inventory of necessities for the living room should include a major seating piece, a lounge chair or two, occasional tables, and bookcases. In addition, imaginative lighting and tree-sized plants will fill in the bare spots and empty corners much more effectively than furniture.

Dark walls and a lighted built-in bookcase contribute to the serene mood of this living room in a Greenwich Village townhouse.
PHOTO: JAMES MATHEWS

COLOR DYNAMICS

COLOR CAN BE A FORMIDABLE decorating tool if used creatively. Like a magician, it can perform optical tricks, transform and alter space—or our visual impression of it, which amounts to the same thing. Nothing affects a room or a person's response to it quite as much as color. It is the first thing one notices and the last thing one remembers.

Color has such an impact on all of us because it is capable of carrying a positive or negative charge. It is a force that affects us emotionally, altering our mood as much as it visually alters our space. Certain colors make us feel content and relaxed, physically attractive, and emotionally vibrant. Conversely, other colors, especially if they are used in jarring combinations, can make us feel tense, anxious, and depressed.

We respond to color in a personal way, depending upon our own psychological makeup. Color is a relative phenomenon; no two people see the same color in precisely the same way. Some people find dark walls restful while others find them depressing. Most people find the quieter shades of blue, green, beige, and off-white soothing, yet the room that uses these tones exclusively runs the risk of appearing too dull and must be enlivened with accent colors.

Light, as Isaac Newton, the English scientist, discovered in the seventeenth century, is the source of all color. Observing that light passing through a glass prism reflected a rainbow of color on the wall, he concluded that color was a result of sunlight rather than a quality inherent in the object itself. When a beam of light strikes a surface, some of the waves are absorbed while others bounce off of it. The waves that are not absorbed determine the color we perceive. Each color in the spectrum has a particular wavelength; the bluish hues contain the shortest wavelengths, while the reddish hues have the longest. Light, then, strongly affects color. A given color will appear completely different under varying light conditions, say, when viewed in broad daylight as opposed to incandescent or fluorescent lighting. A colored fabric can change dramatically depending upon its texture and whether it absorbs or reflects light.

Whether it is the vibration of the light waves or some other mechanism yet to be discovered which determines how color affects us has been the subject of much research. Myth and legend are gradually receiving factual confirmation. Instinctive reactions toward color are proving to be true in scientific experiments. Some colors have tradi-

A floral pattern in beige and plum not only carpets the floors but is also repeated as the upholstery print on the settee and chaise longue. The Madrid apartment was designed by Jay Steffy.
PHOTO: JAY STEFFY

67

tionally been associated with energy and heat. We speak of warm colors (red, yellow, orange) and of cool ones (blue and green). Red excites, stimulates, and arouses our appetites. That's why many restaurants are predominantly red. It is the color of action, even of aggression; one speaks of "seeing red," for instance. Yellow is linked to sunlight and sunny days. It is the color we associate with hope and cheerfulness. Blue, the color of both the sky and the ocean, is restful, soothing, recuperative. Hospital rooms are often painted a soft blue. Green, another cool color, is refreshing and invigorating, like spring leaves or "a breath of fresh air." Notice how many menthol cigarettes are packaged in green to emphasize the idea of refreshment.

We also think of color as possessing such physical properties as weight (heavy or light), or in terms of its relationship to sound (soft or loud), and even to smell (fresh). Dr. Max Lüscher devised a color test which has been used as a major diagnostic aid by psychologists and physicians ever since it was first introduced in 1947 at the International Congress of Psychologists in Switzerland. As a result of his experiments, he found that color could determine personality patterns and could even disclose ailments in their early stages; it could also be used for purposes of vocational guidance. Even more interesting is the role color plays in stimulating or depressing our nervous systems. People who were exposed to pure red for varying lengths of time displayed a marked rise in blood pressure, respiration, and heartbeat, while individuals exposed to pure blue experienced a decrease in blood pressure, heartbeat, and breathing. Lüscher's experiments also indicated that a person's muscular reaction is faster under red lights than under green lights and, moreover, that people left in red rooms were inclined to overestimate both the amount of time that passed and the room's temperature, while those individuals who were confined to blue rooms underestimated both time and temperature. So powerful is one's reaction to color that when London's Blackfriars Bridge, a gloomy, black structure, was repainted a bright green, the formerly high incidence of suicide declined.

Given the psychological and physiological effects of color, it would be logical to assume that all rooms should be painted in the calm blue end of the spectrum. Color schemes for rooms do not work that way, however. Psychologists have theorized that extroverts prefer the warmer and more vibrant colors of the spectrum, while introverts are drawn to cooler and more subtle shades. There are, however, so many tints, tones, and shades of a single color that even those selected from the warmer end of the spectrum can be calmed down just as blues and greens can be intensified. Any color can be reduced to a light tint, juxtaposed with other colors that tend to neutralize it, or muted to appear as a neutral shade. Every color in the rainbow can be intensified or softened, from glowing neon red to dull gray.

In addition, we depend upon color to perform optical tricks with problem spaces. Color can accentuate a room's best features, such as handsome moldings around doorways and windows, or minimize unattractive structural elements. Limiting the use of color to the "safe" end of the spectrum denies its important decorative function. Colors are frequently referred to as "advancing" or "receding." The bright, hot colors, such as those found in the red-orange range of the spectrum, advance; walls painted these colors seem to come forward. A room whose walls are painted red or orange might appear smaller than it really is; conversely, darker colors tend to recede, thus causing the walls of a room to fade away.

The type of lighting used and whether the paint has a glossy or matte finish both have a tremendous effect and can even reverse the above rule. For instance, a charcoal brown wall illuminated by a bright spot of light will certainly emerge as an important focal point. That particular wall, regardless of its dark color, will tend to advance. Because color is light, or its reflection, lighting determines just how you will react to a room painted a certain color. (More on this subject may be found in the chapter on lighting.)

The direction a room faces may determine what color it should be painted. In northern climates, where winters are long, rooms that face north will acquire a sunny ambiance if painted in the warm, red-yellow end of the spectrum; conversely, rooms facing due south may need a dose of the cooler tones from the blue-green range to visually lower the temperature during the hot summer months. These basic principles need not be applied with an iron hand, but they should be kept in mind when working out a color scheme.

Changing Tastes in Color

Taste in color has changed dramatically in the past two decades. Pictures of interiors dating back to the 1950s illustrate how far we have come in accepting color in our everyday lives. Interiors of that time seem timid and bland; their colors, mostly tints of light blues and greens, appear watered down in comparison to our color-saturated schemes of today. Exposure to vibrant color permeates our lives; we encounter it in graphics, in modern art, in colorful advertising, in fashion, and in color TV. People today prefer clear, strong, brilliant color to the insipid tints of yesteryear. We have become more sophisticated in our color preferences.

Designers have characteristically been in the vanguard of coloristic experiments, boldly juxtaposing colors never thought to be compatible and adventurously mixing them in new combinations. We find color today in the most unexpected places: on floors, for instance, which have been bleached and painted or stenciled with a pattern; ceilings are painted in vibrant colors, such as yellow or blue, while the walls remain white. The discovery of new applications for color has contributed significantly to the excitement in interior design.

The color palette itself has broadened. Neutral colors include a whole range of new shades. When we think of a neutral color, the most obvious one that comes to mind is beige and its relatives, oyster white, greige (a gray beige), and gray. Few of us think of red as a neutral color, but today it is often considered one. The function of neutrals is to blend in with many other colors and certain of the newer, deeper tones—plum, forest green, sooty grays, charcoal brown, midnight blues, which are all part of the new family of neutral colors—have greatly expanded the range of background colors for today's rooms. Think of a deep burgundy red and how compatible it is with so many other colors, from pinks to hot orange.

Accent colors, too, are now bolder and brighter. Their names suggest their vibrancy: canary yellow, lipstick red, acid green, electric blue. These are best used in small doses, and are surrounded by white or neutral colors to "defuse" their powerful charge.

Colors Have Names

To simplify our discussion of color, let's clear up the question of terminology. Colors are grouped into families. A single, specific color, which includes all of its lighter and darker variations, is called a *hue*. The primary color red, for instance, is a hue; if that red is diluted with white, a lighter color, or *tint*, results. Any hue diluted with white is called a tint. When a hue is mixed with gray to darken it, it is called a *shade*. In general, tints are light colors and shades are darker colors of a particular color family or hue. Color *value* refers to its lightness or darkness; the dullness or brightness of a color, or its concentration of pure pigment, is called its *chroma* or *intensity*. The primary reason for learning these terms is to be able to recognize the incredible range of a single color. For example, to recognize that aquamarine is a tint of teal blue is a guarantee that the colors will be harmonious when used together because they are all part of the same color family.

The intensity, or chroma, of a color also helps to determine where to use it. Strong colors, or those of high chroma, are best used in small doses as accent colors, whereas deep shades of a color can give a room a ponderous feeling if they are not relieved by tints. Colors of light intensity make a room appear spacious and airy, but they require a contrast of either darker shades or high chroma to avoid monotony. Neutral shades are great mixers and are compatible with many other colors of higher chroma. The color scheme that alternates between light and dark or dull and bright values invigorates a room.

Creating a Color Scheme

Color schemes do not have to be complex to be successful. Careful analysis will disclose the fact that rooms need surprisingly little formal color since so many colors are predetermined—the wood floors and wood furniture, for instance, or the various shades of green of plants. Most highly successful color schemes utilize no more than three colors, a neutral background, and two accent colors. One hue can be employed for an entire room by varying the patterns and textures.

Rooms can generally be divided into three basic color units:

1. The major color area, or background: walls and floors.

2. The secondary color area: the upholstery of the major seating group and the window treatment.

3. The accent color(s): small occasional chairs, pillows, and accessories.

Colors are selected from among the most neutral to the most brilliant hues, depending upon the square footage that they will occupy in the room. Most designers prefer to keep the background, or major color area, neutral. The secondary area, which includes the upholstery of the major seating group and the window treatment, can utilize patterns or colors of greater brilliance. The accent colors, which are the hottest shades of all, are used in the smallest areas. Although this rule of thumb generates the most livable schemes, many designers reject these guidelines with impunity. The novice color planner, however, will find them both safe and useful to follow.

A color chart consisting of swatches of fabric to be used in the room can serve as a convenient way of testing the harmony of the overall scheme. Swatches of the proposed colors and fabrics are pasted onto a white sheet of paper. The size of the swatches should be relative to the area they will occupy in the actual room: the background color should be the largest swatch; the secondary color or fabrics should be approximately half that size; while the accent colors may be represented by small dots of color. Working up such a color chart enables the planner to experiment by adding or subtracting additional colors or fabrics. It's a little like wardrobe planning, where the clothes to be worn are laid out on the bed and tested for their total effect. With a color plan, one can tell at a glance whether the colors are compatible in terms of surface area and combinations desired.

Here are a few helpful hints when working with color:

FLOORS: Keep this large area neutral. Choose a low-key color that mixes well with colors at both ends of the spectrum—the red-oranges and the blue-greens. Several possible choices are sandy beige, oatmeal, cinnamon, russet, olive drab, slate gray, and brown.

WALLS: Since walls take up the most space, this area should likewise be neutral or low in color intensity. If beige is selected, choose a beige with a hint of the basic hue of the overall scheme—khaki for yellows and oranges rather than a pink beige, for instance. If the carpet color is vibrant, don't introduce another wholly different color for the walls. Boldly painted walls require tempering with a neutral floor surface.

UPHOLSTERY: Here is the place to try brighter colors, patterns, and textures. If carpet and walls are plain, upholstery can be patterned. Mix and match chair and sofa fabrics in solids and prints; a sofa might be covered in a multicolored printed fabric, with the chairs picking up individual colors as solids.

CURTAINS AND DRAPERIES: If everything else is plain, the draperies might be patterned, the design reflecting one of the colors from the wall, carpet, or upholstery. The more colors which are repeated in the drapery pattern the better. That's why it's best to start with the printed fabric rather than the other way around. Problem windows should be played down; they could either be treated as a soft wall of fabric or covered with vertical blinds.

ACCESSORIES: Pillows, paintings, and other objects in the room may legitimately "shock" with color. Use brighter hues for chair cushions, pillows, posters, paintings, lamp bases, etc.

Where to Use Color

The best color schemes are usually the result of either an idea, concept, or vision of how the room will be or an emotional response to the space itself. Often, the size of a room and its distinctive architecture suggest an appropriate decorative scheme. Whether the room is naturally light or dark is also a factor. Pale walls and ceilings, especially if they are painted white, tend to brighten a poorly lit space. Whether or not a room has any interesting architectural features worth playing up also affects the overall scheme. A neutral wall is often the best background for interesting furniture, paintings, or assorted collections. A bank of bay windows overlooking a garden may suggest that the walls be painted a mint green tint with moldings outlined in crisp white. A fireplace with an ornately carved marble mantel may be begging for walls painted a deep sooty gray to frame its sumptuous carving. On the other hand, even though a nondescript apartment in a high-rise building may have nothing architecturally distinctive about it, its windows may provide a fabulous view of the city's rooftops. Whatever colors are eventually selected for that space, the view must still stand out in the completed room when the front door is opened. Soft and neutral colors would not compete with the city's twinkling lights.

The size of a room is often a major factor in deciding upon a color scheme. Small or narrow spaces which are normally devoid of daylight—hallways, foyers, bar alcoves, elevator wells, corridors—lend themselves remarkably well to dark or intense colors. These spaces can afford to be dramatically dark because people usually do not stay in them for any great length of time. Dark or intensely colored rooms are particularly theatrical when the adjoining spaces are large and bright. A tiny room may be just the place to go all out with color—scarlet, plum, russet, forest green, orange, or bright yellow. Entering a small room painted a deep or brilliant color makes one aware that it is small. But the movement from such a space into a large, brightly illuminated room dispels any feeling of being trapped. This juxtaposition is important.

One designer described a tiny, totally red room he had designed for a client who wanted a morning room in which to sip coffee while opening the mail as resembling "the inside of a lacquered box." Walls, carpeting, upholstered settee, and chairs were all done up in a brilliant Chinese red. A bright red room can be very exciting for certain individuals. One writer painted her home office a bright red-orange because she claimed that it revved her up and improved her writing.

Many interior designers advocate a color balance in a house or apartment. Light, sunny spaces should be balanced by dark, intimate spaces. Frequently, the living room is the sunniest room, full of subtle color, with sunlight playing on fabrics and textures, filtering through plants, and bringing the whole room to life. But it is also marvelous to have one secluded place—be it a library, dining room, or den—that is cozy and dark.

The idea for a color scheme can originate, not only with the architecture or size of a room, but with a fabric swatch, a bit of wallpaper, a painting, a picture from a book or magazine, or even from the design in a rug or the pattern in draperies that will be used in the room. An unusual wallpaper, big enough to hang in the center hallway of a large suburban house, can set the scheme for the entire lower level of that house. One color from the paper might reappear in the living room in the form of solid colored walls; a much lighter tint might serve as the wall color for the dining room; yet another accent color from the wallpaper might cover the walls of the library. A person standing in the center hallway could thus see the progression of color and space; despite this variety, a basic strain of color can be seen to run through all the rooms.

Sequences of spaces within the house or apartment are important factors to bear in mind in color planning. The colors of adjoining rooms or rooms that are traversed to get to other rooms should be considered as a unit. Avoid a cacophony of coloristic effects; a basic thread should weave in and out of the interrelated spaces.

Pattern and Texture

Pattern and texture are important ingredients in any color scheme. The use of patterned fabrics and wallpaper in a room is still a controversial issue. Many modern designers feel that the less they see of pattern the better, although print fabrics and wallpaper are effective in the traditionally styled room. Whether or not to use patterned fabric and wallpaper depends upon the size and location of the room. A living room is no place for a large, decorative wallpaper. An overpowering pattern tends to make the space look busy and visually jarring. A living room ought to be easy on the eyes and inviting. The people in it should be the room's most obvious element. Conversely, patterned fabrics, such as a colorful chintz spread for the sofa or the same fabric used as draperies, can be highly effective in giving a room a sense of warmth.

Country accents enliven the city kitchen designed by Jay Hyde Crawford and Anthony Tortora in Manhattan.
PHOTO: PAUL VANEYRE

73

Small rooms or tiny areas—such as the ceiling and walls above the tops of kitchen cabinets—are good places to use wallpaper. Rooms that are used infrequently are also good candidates for patterned wallpaper. Bathrooms are fine for all kinds of small prints. The size of the pattern or design is important. There is a wide range of wallpaper patterns, running the gamut from large, insistent designs to tiny, small-scaled geometrics, narrow stripes, and linen textures, which are subtle enough to lend texture rather than pattern to a scheme. Trend-setting patterns should be avoided. Their popularity may wear thin in a year and the room will look as dated as last season's hemline. If a pattern is to be utilized, it should be selected first, with the color for walls, trim, and ceiling cued to it. Otherwise, one will search in vain for a pattern which blends in well with a desired scheme and an established wall color. This advice will save endless hours of hunting.

Texture can provide a decorative scheme with all the visual interest of pattern without running the risk of becoming jarring or distracting. Texture has a wonderfully subtle richness—from the silky shimmer of satin or the nubbly look of rough wool to the krinkly feel of chintz or polished cotton. Think of texture as being three dimensional and use it to create contrasting surfaces—hard/soft, smooth/rough, shiny/dull, translucent/opaque. These qualities are all part of the vitality of texture.

Texture affects and alters color. Color changes dramatically depending upon whether it absorbs or reflects light. Rough weaves tend to deepen a color because of the large number of shadows which are cast. Smooth, shiny surfaces and weaves with a sheen or glaze reflect more of the light waves; colors thus appear lighter, more lustrous.

Light also affects the way we see color. Occasionally, colors that match under daylight conditions do not seem to match under incandescent or fluorescent light. Because of these variables, all color samples selected for a room should be tested under the light conditions existing in that room. A color scheme must appear harmonious under a variety of light conditions, from natural daylight to the artificial light of evening. Daylight is the most flattering light of all for most colors and textiles. Incandescent light plays up the yellow and red spectrum but tends to dull the blues and violets. Fluorescent light, especially the old tube types, reverse the effect by dulling red tones and enhancing blues and greens; newer fluorescents, however, are color corrected and give off a light closer to incandescent light than ever before. It's important to remember that a physical color match is not always a good visual match.

The reflective qualities of surface textures greatly affect the color we see. Glossy, enameled surfaces appear lighter than flat, or matte, painted surfaces. The former reflects more light while the latter absorbs more. Any seamstress working at home has experienced the quixotic qualities of corduroy and velvet; swatches of the exact same fabric appear to possess two entirely different colors depending upon the light hitting the fabric's nap or pile. The same thing holds true for shiny or matte surfaces of the same color. Bright light falling on textures at an angle enhances their dimensional qualities; diffused light tends to flatten textures.

Twenty-five Foolproof Color Schemes

Here are twenty-five foolproof color schemes. Colors within each scheme are interchangeable, i.e., the wall color can be used as the carpet color and the scheme will still work. When patterned fabrics are to be used, the color listed for sofa or draperies in the scheme should predominate.

Walls	Carpet	Sofa or Draperies	Accents
Silver blue	Deep sky blue	Curry yellow	Black, gold, white
Lettuce	Khaki	Spring green	Emerald, purple, yellow
Chestnut brown	Pale beige	Chinese yellow	Red, orange, white
White	Black	Vermillion	Cream, brass
Tomato	Oatmeal	Black and white	Faded coral
Melon	Slate	Tangerine	Black, white
Yellow	Slate	Black	Lemon, white
Pearl gray	Dark gray	Bronze gold	White, mint green
White	Black and white	Lime green	Yellow, black
Slate	String	Khaki	Curry yellow, white
Mint green	String	Emerald and white	Gold, emerald
Cornflower blue	Navy blue	Blue and white	Yellow, coral
Khaki	Cinnamon	White	Black, orange
White	Silver gray	Honey gold	Black, brass, cinnamon
White	Black and white	Magenta	Black, red
String	Forest green	Beige and natural	Emerald, bronze gold
Orange	Slate	White	Cinnamon brown, curry
Tan	Chestnut brown	Scarlet	White, hot pink
Lemon	Slate	Green and white	Cinnamon
Cream	Cinnamon	Cream	Black, curry yellow
Curry yellow	Walnut	Yellow and white	Black, brass
Pearl gray	Coral	White	Purple, magenta, black
Walnut	Cream	Cream	Brass, magenta, curry
Ivory	Dull copper	Ivory	Pink, copper, bronze
Melon	Russett	Ivory	Black, gold, red

LIGHTING

LIGHTING IS DECORATING's most effective mood modifier. Notice how theater lighting effects can create a sense of excitement, shift one's attention, single out a character, upset the public or soothe it, create a mood of sadness and desolation, or even physically change the space, time of day, or season of the year, not by playing with the scenery, but merely by flicking a light switch.

To achieve such a range of light effects, the theater technician relies solely upon dimmers, the width of the light beam, and on color filters. The ability of light to transform space and alter mood is what creative lighting is all about. It is the most recent tool available to the interior designer; new ways to use light in the home appear every day.

Not too many years ago, lighting was thought of in terms of general illumination and foot candles, two technical terms that stressed quantity rather than quality. One designer remembers receiving the following advice from his design school instructor: "If the room needs more light, use a bigger bulb." People bought light fixtures as decorative accessories rather than for the type and amount of light they produced.

This chapter is concerned with the quality of light, what it can do for a room, how to work with it to create atmosphere—not with the esthetics of light fixtures. Regardless of how much money is spent on furniture and accessories, a room will still look dull and boring if the light is poorly situated or too intense. The quality of light, i.e., its tone and intensity and the angle of its beam, can bring out form, texture, and perspective.

After the floor plan and furniture arrangement of a room have been worked out, decide what kind of light to use and where to put it. Traffic patterns have to be determined in advance so that lights do not shine in people's eyes as they move through the space. It's necessary to anticipate future changes in the furniture arrangement to determine how they will affect the light placement. Once the lights are up, they are there to stay.

The biggest change in lighting design has occurred in the area of fixtures; there has been a marked trend away from conventional table lamps and toward recessed ceiling lights, floor cans, strip lights, and track lights. Light effects can be divided into general types, each possessing a unique quality of its own. Because they lend character to a space, they are collectively termed atmospheric lighting.

Glossy white walls reflect the glow of lighting in an apartment designed by Joseph D'Urso.
PHOTO: PETER AARON

FLOODS: Floodlights are used to whitewash walls over a wide area, thus eliminating clearly defined edges. This light effect is favored by art galleries to uniformly illuminate a wall of paintings. Floods are also called wallwashers because of the wash of uniform light they produce.

SPOTS: Spotlights have a narrower beam, usually no more than a 30-degree angle. The edges of the area they illuminate are more sharply defined. The light effect they produce resembles a circular pool. Spots, as their name implies, are used to highlight specific areas or objects.

STRIP LIGHTING: This type of illumination consists of a strip of light produced by tubular bulbs connected end to end. Frequently used behind a ledge or shelf, or beneath a seating platform, strip lighting creates an intimate, uniform light effect that outlines the length of the surface. Strip lighting, especially when dimmed, produces a dramatic effect. A cheaper, and equally effective, solution involves the use of a string of Christmas tree lights hidden behind a cove or cornice.

UPLIGHTS: Uplights are tall, can-like fixtures or small spotlights that rest on the floor, casting their beam up to the ceiling. Uplights produce a shower of dramatic light and shadow when placed under tall plants. They can also be beamed up at sculpture, placed under tables, or placed in corners. Designer John Saladino has achieved a beautiful lighting effect by beaming an uplight onto a painted cymbal. It casts a soft, reflected glow in the room, made even more dramatic because the light source appears to be invisible.

FRAMING PROJECTORS: These light fixtures, as their name implies, have a built-in focusing device. They are also equipped with louvers or templates that can be adjusted to cast a sharply defined beam in square, circular, or rectangular shapes. When it is beamed at a painting, the framing projector makes the former appear to be backlighted. Unlike the other types of beams, these produce no spillover of light. Because framing projectors are sophisticated lighting devices, they are expensive, selling for $100 or more.

DIMMERS: No sophisticated lighting system can dispense with a dimmer switch. Even if it is the only change made in a room's lighting arrangement, the effect is tremendous. Dimmers are nifty devices which expand the potential of all light fixtures. The ability to dim or brighten a room can create a variety of moods within a single space. If a room has more than one circuit and several light sources, the effects which can be produced are almost as varied as those found in a theatrical set.

Where to Use Light

When we are struck by a room's beauty, it is the total effect that impresses us. The eye does not isolate specific elements—the type of furniture and its arrangement; the architectural features of the space itself; the richness of textures or colors—although all of these elements contribute to a total sense of beauty. It is the contrast between highlights and shadows, between powerful lights falling on rich textures plus the angle at which the light is cast, that makes all the difference between a pleasant room and a spectacular one. The question is: how do we make light perform its magic?

An understanding of the creative uses of light is something that can only be developed gradually. The best way to develop it is through experimentation. The angle of a light source is crucial in determining the effect it will produce. For instance, indirect lighting is the best kind of illumination to live with. It is not as harsh as direct lighting, since it involves light bounced back from a wall onto which it was projected. Indirect lighting flatters people; the absence of shadows plays down circles under the eyes and flattens wrinkles. Conversely, lights shining down from above directly onto a person's face are both uncomfortable to sit under and highly unflattering. (Remember this fact when planning the lighting arrangement for the dining room table.) Lights should never be aimed into the eyes. (Remember the scene in the gangster movie with the glaring lights shining directly into the prisoner's eyes during the interrogation?)

The lighting arrangement is intimately tied to furniture and art placement: reading lights are needed by the sofa and chairs; spots are effective over works of art and important objects; general illumination is required for work areas; a wallwasher will certainly dramatize an area. Choose a fixture for its function. Clamp-type lamps with a flexible arm similar to those used on an architect's drafting table make excellent work and desk lights. Floor and table lamps depend upon the decorative scheme, although chrome and brass lights blend best with both modern and traditional furniture. Most popular of all are the flexible goose-neck floor lamps, copied from the doctor's examining-room lamp. Other related styles have swiveling arms and telescopic posts to direct the light right over the area. For reading purposes, a light fixture requires a 75- or 100-watt bulb which is properly shielded and placed one or two feet away from the reading or work material. This is the most basic type of light and consequently leaves little room for experimentation.

Mood lighting is an entirely different matter. Here there is ample room for experimentation and creative expression. The most versatile atmospheric lighting should come from several places; lighting might be situated overhead; uplights could be placed on the floor or directed at a painting or a piece of sculpture; a hanging lamp would be ideal over a game table. When the source of light is hidden, the effect is wonderfully mysterious. A mixture of different types of light can be dramatic; some light sources should be cool, others warm.

Certain bulbs tend to produce warmer tones. Regular R40, 150-watt floods and spots create warm tones, while Krypton-filled bulbs produce cooler tones with more blue in them. Clear bulbs usually have a a cooler tone. When this kind of light is aimed at large plants, it creates a wonderfully fresh effect. Dimming a light affects its color. Dimmed light is warmer, more intimate. It looks very much like candlelight.

Architectural forms are highlighted by light beams aimed from the side. Deep shadows accentuate their outlines. A concentrated spot singles out details and accessories. When the latter are brightly lit and the surrounding area is left in shadow, the illuminated object becomes more vivid. Sidelighting a wall frieze or a texture emphasizes them by throwing the surface into high relief. To emphasize anything at all, aim a light at it.

Several areas of interest, or focal points, can be created in this

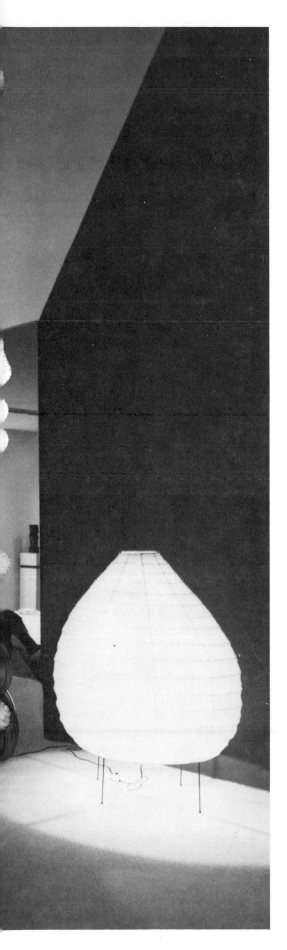

manner. For instance, you might shine a light at the African mask over the fireplace or down at the plants in the corners of the room. Spotlight another piece of sculpture, a painting, or a wall niche. Then dim some areas while brightening others. The room will exude atmosphere.

Rooms with a view of the city lights are particularly difficult to illuminate. At night, light in the room reflects off the windows and obliterates the glorious view. Framing projectors which have no spillover and give out very low reflected illumination keep the light in its place —on the art and off the windows. Living rooms whose windows overlook a landscaped garden have a similar problem: at night, the window walls become black holes; outdoor lights illuminating the trees bring the garden view back indoors, even at night.

Track Lighting

To perform these varied functions, the lighting system has to be versatile. A most versatile system to install and use is track lighting. A recent innovation, it is one reason for the growing sophistication of home lighting. It makes the manipulation of light easy because there are several types of fixtures and countless ways to position them.

That's the good news. The bad news is that such variety leaves room for error when choosing between competitive systems and during installation. Ask yourself the following questions when selecting a track system:

1. Which system offers the greatest number of fixtures that can perform several functions?
2. How many circuits are available in a single track?
3. Which system has the finest quality fixtures? (This is difficult to determine without actually working with the system—talk to someone who is familiar with various types of fixtures or who has actually used them.)
4. How complicated is the system to install?
5. Can a fixture be switched from one circuit to another?
6. How reliable are the connecting elements?
7. Are special fixtures, such as framing projectors, available?

Basically, what you ought to find out is, first, whether or not the system possesses enough fixtures to supply the variety of lighting you presently require and will want in the future and, second, whether or not the track has the flexibility necessary to control these fixtures independently. Fixtures are not interchangeable among different brands.

The Noguchi paper floor lamp sets up a pool of light in this apartment designed by John Saladino. Overhead are track lights.
PHOTO: JAMES MATHEWS

The following are the basic types of fixtures a track should offer:

Floods, from 40 watts to 250 watts, with grids, or barn doors, to shield against glare; this last accessory is optional, but will prove very helpful when needed. Also optional are units with hooks that accept color filters.

Spots; same considerations as floods for wattage and accessories.

Framing projectors possessing sufficient power, depending on where they will be used, to cast a beam large enough to encompass whatever they are intended to frame. Also, make sure that if circular shapes are needed, there is a template or other device to project them; not all brands of projectors are capable of casting circular beams.

Tungsten-halogen lamps of high output per watt for special purposes. The most common use is to illuminate plants; plant lovers with dark apartments like to give their plants extra light during the day. Tungsten-halogen bulbs provide a much higher degree of illumination per watt than regular incandescent lamps.

Tracks with at least two circuits should be selected; it would be highly impractical to use a separate track for each type of fixture. This will permit you to turn some lights off while others remain on or are dimmed. Framing projectors, for instance, work best alone or with very dim lighting. When shining grow lights, you obviously don't want all the other lights running up the meter; consequently, you require one more circuit.

While several circuits per track may be necessary, too many could become a source of trouble. Simple things usually work better and create fewer complications than complex ones. Note whether shifting the fixture from one circuit to another is a simple operation or if it requires steps involving adaptors, more contacts that may not work, or procedures which are easily forgotten or which may lead to breakage if not followed to the letter. Ask the salesman if connectors between segments of track always work and whether the contacts are firm; nothing is more maddening than installing the tracks and screwing them into the ceiling, only to find that the connections are not sound.

Competitive prices for track lighting should not be your prime consideration. The largest expense is incurred in the installation. The physical differences between the American-made systems are not that significant once all the costs have been totalled. Don't sacrifice flexibility or quality to save $70 on a $600 job.

The shape and color of the fixture should not be an overriding concern, either. Track lighting is intended to provide the right type of light for the right place. Few people are really aware of the light source. All manufacturers offer white tracks or lamps that are quite unobtrusive. Besides, functional objects justify their own existence; the eye compensates for their presence.

Where to Place Tracks

While a track possesses the added flexibility of permitting the lamp to be placed anywhere along its length, the positioning of the track itself is important; moving a lamp in one direction or another doesn't compensate for clumsy, haphazard track placement. For example, lamps positioned on tracks mounted too close to the wall cast long shadows that magnify every wall imperfection; they also tend to shine in people's faces. Conversely, lights positioned on tracks mounted too far from the wall produce too much spillover. The light source, again, will shine from side angles.

The general rule for apartments with eight-foot ceilings is: place the track a distance of two feet from the wall. This will create a suitable forty-five degree angle for the fixture. If space limitations make it necessary to err from this rule of thumb, err on the far side. A fixture with barn doors will screen off most of the glare. Unfortunately, there is no solution for those long shadows that play up every minor wall imperfection when the track is mounted too close to the wall.

Consider all reflecting surfaces when positioning the track. To illuminate something near a mirror or window, keep the track as close to the mirror or window as possible. If this is not feasible, position the track so that the reflection can only be seen from a point in the room that is rarely frequented, i.e., one where there is little traffic. This can be achieved by illuminating the object directly overhead or at a very oblique angle.

Hiding a track system's wiring is a problem. Chipping through the concrete slab of ceilings in high-rise buildings is a nightmare. A much simpler solution involves the use of a wire-mold conduit. This molding comes in different sizes so as to accept wires of different gauges. Running the wire-mold close to the room's natural ceiling or beam lines and painting it the same color as the wall once it has been installed renders the wires almost invisible. The wire-mold system also includes boxes for switches and dimmers which are easy to install.

Think ahead when selecting a dimmer switch. Instead of loading the dimmer to its specified capacity, leave enough room to add more fixtures to a circuit. Total the wattage of all the bulbs in the fixtures and reserve another hundred watts for additional fixtures; this figure should reflect the minimum amount of wattage for the dimmer selected.

With lighting, you can afford to be bold. The consequences of track-related errors will not involve even a fraction of the expense of, say, repainting a house when the scheme doesn't work. Many fixtures, particularly those designed for use with tracks, accept color filters. For about $2 a color filter can change the tint and alter the mood of an entire room. If there is a feature in the room that is interesting, try to enhance it with light. See what it looks like under different light conditions. Try to bring out the best qualities. Never mind if the room's decorative scheme is traditional and the track light is modern—the purpose of light is to bring out the beauty in objects and the room itself. Whatever product best achieves that goal is the product to use.

MONEY MATTERS

*A room can have the simplest
things in it and be the
most elegant place in town.*
David Easton

A bay window in this San Francisco
living room is the background for
a seating banquette. As a capricious
touch, the coffee tables are packing
crates. The room was designed by
John Dickinson.
PHOTO: PETER REED

THE QUESTION EVERYONE SEEMS TO ASK IS: how much does decorating cost? Is it possible to create a beautiful room on a budget, or does it require the bank roll of a shipping magnate? Good design doesn't depend on money; a beautiful room can be tastefully decorated for any amount, large or minuscule. Decorating, like Parkinson's Law costs as much or as little as one wishes to spend. It is really the art of living well, an attitude that we either instinctively possess or have to cultivate. The size of a space, be it a home or apartment, doesn't matter that much, either; a studio-apartment dweller can live as well as the owner of a mansion. People with a zest for living find ways to stamp their places with a sense of style. Conversely, a negative attitude toward life is often expressed in terms of dreary interiors or indifferent surroundings.

Good design is the result of a selective eye. Only after the eye has been trained to "see" the beauty of an object—a chair, a table, a vase, a lamp—and is able to judge its esthetic merits can one begin to save money on decorating. What the eye cannot discern for itself will have to be purchased as a service. We pay a designer to make design decisions which we cannot make ourselves.

This service is expensive. Many well-known designers have stated that they cannot decorate a room for under $10,000. This is their low figure. By the time they evaluate a room and make such structural changes as shifting doorways and electrical outlets, resurfacing floors, relocating walls, installing the decorative background, i.e., putting up mirrors, painting, and carpeting—all done by professional workmen— a considerable sum has been spent. Next comes furniture, draperies, art, and accessories. It adds up rapidly.

When we hire a designer, we pay him for his familiarity with craftsmen, contractors, and resources; we also pay him for his experience, his imagination—and his selective eye. If we knew what he knows, then we could design and decorate interiors ourselves. Saving or spending money on decoration depends upon the way we envision the design possibilities or alternatives of a given space. Because designers are specifically trained to do this, they save enormous sums on decoration—usually on their own apartments rather than those of clients; they would lose money on the job if they always economized for clients.

Designers delight in mentioning where and how they acquired a particularly pleasing object in their apartment or house; they usually bought it for a pittance and enjoy recounting the bargain. Actually, present tastes have veered away from expensive status symbols toward simple, natural, primitive objects where the hand of the craftsman is clearly evident—baskets, natural clay pots, or small bamboo tables from China or Japan. Objects that cost very little yet are interesting or amusing, or items that have been picked up in unusual places, are today's status symbols. Why the sudden reversal? One explanation is that to have found a treasure at a low price proves that the owner has a sensitive eye; he or she can discern quality where it is least expected.

What Is the Difference Between a Designer and a Decorator?

Up until the 1950s, professionals who planned interiors called themselves decorators and didn't mind the name. Along came the building boom, with office buildings and high-rise apartments rising like mushrooms in urban centers. A need developed for specialized designers with architectural skills to augment the architect's role and finish the interiors. Today, the term decorator generally applies to the professional who deals with the room as it currently exists. (There is, however, no hard-and-fast rule, many decorators like to become involved with architectural changes.) Designers, on the other hand, feel qualified to manipulate the space, remodel it, change it, sculpt it, build in furniture, change windows or floor levels, and develop sophisticated lighting and install it. As designer Joseph D'Urso so aptly put it: "Decorators add; designers subtract from the space."

How Do You Select a Designer or Decorator?

Choosing a designer or decorator is a little like choosing a psychiatrist: there has to be a good rapport, a subtle blending of personalities; client and professional have to be on the same wavelength. There's only one way to locate that special professional and that involves meeting and talking to several. Read specialized magazines, appropriate columns in newspapers, and visit other people's homes. Ask individuals whom you respect for recommendations; write to the local newspaper's home furnishings editor. When the choice has been narrowed down to three or four possible designers, try to personally see and talk to all of them. Ask to see other examples of their work. Discuss your budget freely and openly to avoid any future misunderstandings; if it is very limited, say so. If the designer cannot work within such limited means, he should also be truthful in a tactful manner. The budget should never be left a mystery. Get it out in the open.

Most of the top designers practicing today are available for a one-hour consultation. The going rate is somewhere between $75 and $100. Few people realize what a wealth of information that hour can provide. One young couple signed up for an hour-long consultation with designer John Saladino. Even though their budget was very small, they came away with the basis for a complete room scheme: advice on what kind of furniture to buy; what colors to use; where to place the furniture; and how to save money and plan for the future. The fee is truly a bargain for being permitted to pick the brains of the experts—and thereby saving a houseful of mistakes. Be sure to take along an accurate floor plan for reference during the session—and don't forget to make a list of all those troubling questions.

Setting Up a Budget

It's surprising to discover how many people buy furniture with only the vaguest notion of how much they ought to spend. They shop aimlessly, hoping to see something that appeals to them or inspires them with a decorating idea. They are easy prey for high-pressure salesmen who talk them into buying tasteless furniture. What they should be looking for is well-designed, well-made furniture that fits within their overall decorating plan—and their budget.

A realistic budget takes into account everything that's needed. Anyone who buys furniture or accessories in a piecemeal fashion runs the risk of paying too much for one item and consequently running out of ready cash before any significant decorative scheme has been achieved. When a real treasure comes along (i.e., one worth rearranging the projected expenditures to acquire), this individual feels that he or she doesn't have the funds to grab it.

For anyone starting from scratch, it's important to draw up a two-year plan. The budget must cover all necessities. Only then can one distinguish between the "must haves" and the "can waits." Long-range planning ensures against filling up the house with compromises. Furniture, draperies, and carpeting hang around for a long time; mistakes can be painful reminders for years to come.

One of the first things to determine is whether the space requires structural changes. The budget will have to include them. Relocating a doorway, enlarging a window, and building a bookcase wall are all part of decorating. Obtain estimates from three different contractors and try to decide which would do the best job for the price. Add this figure to the budget.

What do we actually need? Living essentials are relatively simple for most of us: we all require a table for eating purposes plus four chairs for dining; we need a seating unit and/or a sofa and chairs to accommodate anywhere from four to six persons; we need a bed, a storage unit or chest, and bookcases; two rugs, one for the living room and one for the bedroom; a variety of lamps and lighting fixtures; music equipment—that about sums up the minimum furniture requirements for the bachelor, the single woman, or the childless couple. This list could constitute the first year's "must haves." Draw up a tentative budget based upon a realistic notion of what things actually cost. How does it tally with the available funds? If there is a large discrepancy between what things cost and what you plan to spend, a reordering of your priorities is in order—or more creative shopping. (More on this question can be found in the next section.)

The second year's budget should contain more "frills." The latter might include: two more chairs or a sectional unit for the living room; several additional dining-room chairs; a buffet or serving counter; and a desk (if that wasn't previously a "must have" item). This budget should also include all of the nonessential accessories, mirrors, handsome ashtrays, and paintings. The bedroom probably could use more storage pieces, a small armchair or settee, or a work area. By this time, definite needs will have become apparent; these will naturally be met if sufficient cash is available. The important thing is that money will not have been spent in vain. The second year's expenditures should build upon those of the first. It's far too soon to think about upgrading; consequently, those preliminary decisions are worth every bit of soul-searching.

Decorating as an Investment

The foregoing advice was primarily intended for the family with limited funds. Every budget, however, is not necessarily as limited. Those with a nest egg to invest would be well advised to spend it on their homes. The stock market is fickle, while silver, fine art, and antiques are more stable investments. They, too, have their peaks and valleys, but they consistently provide enjoyment day after day. Unlike stock certificates yellowing in a bank vault, a painting is viewed daily; likewise, a fine French commode or a Queen Anne highboy pleases the eye with its rich patina, a quality acquired over a number of years of handling and use.

Purchasing antiques that will retain their monetary value is—like playing the stock market—best left to the experts. Investing, whether it be in antiques or stocks, is generally a risky business. One can get stung by paying too much for a piece of questionable quality, by not recognizing when a piece has been altered or restored, or, even worse, by purchasing an outright fake. It takes years in the trade to recognize such chicaneries. (Some dedicated novices devote much scholarly research to the study of antiques and become extremely knowledgeable.) The reputable antique dealer and/or knowledgeable decorator are the best safeguards.

There is a distinct advantage in furnishing your interiors with antiques. New furniture—and that includes reproductions—is relatively worthless the day after it is purchased, regardless of how much it originally cost. Even an automobile has a higher resale value. Antiques, on the other hand, remain quite stable in price. If you decide to redecorate or totally change a scheme, the chances are that your antique furniture will still be worth as much—if not more—than when you purchased it a year or so ago. Of course, the quality of the piece must be exceptional and the price paid must be worth the value. Reputable dealers will often buy back their own pieces—yet another advantage of dealing with them in the first place.

People who furnish their interiors with antiques should be aware of the care and attention they require. Upholstered pieces need occasional tightening, regluing of joints, rewebbing, and refilling of cushions. Chests require similar care, in addition to frequent polishing to keep the wood from drying out. European antiques have a tendency to craze and crack because of the differences in humidity levels between the continent and America. They will therefore require a seasoning process in order to adjust to the new climate—once again, this falls within the domain of the professional.

Because provenance is so important a factor in the resale of an antique, you should always demand a note or invoice that clearly states an object's provenance. The bill or invoice should describe the nature of the antique, its age, the factory or place of origin, and its true condition (i.e., whether or not it has been restored). Such a bill is invaluable should the piece ever have to be returned—as well as for tax purposes. It is an essential document in any resale procedure. This holds true for all types of original art as well, including paintings, oriental rugs, antique china, and silver.

Modern art, unlike antiques, has not been around long enough to estimate its true investment potential. There are, of course, towering giants in this field, artists ranging from Picasso to Andy Warhol, whose works represent gilt-edged investments. These artists have a proven track record; anyone who can afford to purchase their works already knows what these items are worth. There are, on the other hand, hundreds of young, talented artists whose work remains an unknown quantity. Purchasing a painting by one of these artists as an investment certainly involves some degree of risk—one can end up with either a meteoric appreciation or none at all. Always purchase a painting or piece of sculpture because of its personal appeal. That way, regardless of the degree of appreciation, the painting or sculpture will be a source of constant pleasure.

Most of us probably fall somewhere between the prince and the pauper. We have to watch our purchases yet we can still afford an occasional splurge (especially if the projected budget incorporates this possibility). Even antiques of less than superb quality have a given resale value. You needn't purchase only the finest antiques to realize a modest return on your investment. All true antiques are worth something. A "new" antique sells for about the same price as a good reproduction. How do they differ? A reproduction was manufactured yesterday. However, reproducing fine eighteenth-century furniture is hardly a new activity; it has been going on for at least a hundred years. Take American Colonial furniture, for example. When this nation celebrated its centennial in 1876, the reproduction of Early American furniture styles was very much in vogue. Today, as the nation celebrates its bicentennial, those reproductions are a hundred years old, antiques in their own right. They are not, however, as valuable as the pieces they were modeled upon, those true Early American Windsor chairs and blanket chests, which are now over two hundred years old and still appreciating in value. Nevertheless, they have acquired a patina as a result of age and use that cannot be copied. Thus, the "new" antique has more charm than a brand-new reproduction. As a result of increased mechanization and inferior materials, today's furniture reproductions lack that distinctive, mellow aura which can only come with age.

Some people still entertain the mistaken notion that everything they put into their homes has to be expensive, that they should not mingle pedigreed objects with humbler ones. This just isn't so. True, some houses are filled solely with objects of superb quality—but these instances are rare. (These homes also run the risk of appearing obsessively stuffy and formal.) The "perfect" room is often rather dull. The greatest ingredient a room possesses is its individual personality. Rooms fail to please when they lack a sense of daring. A mixture of inexpensive things, say, some great thrift-shop finds, with established, gilt-edged investments is exciting and reflects a personal choice. All good rooms possess that subjective, personal touch. Be bold and adventurous; mix periods as well as price tags to create truly spirited schemes.

Designer David Easton believes that every room needs one wonderful piece of—something. It might be an antique French commode, a handsome lacquered secretary, or even a beautiful, rare, and expensive basket. This object gives the room an immediate allure—even when the rest of the furnishings are tasteful yet budget-priced. "Like a rich aunt or a good family name," says Mr. Easton, "it carries a boor a long way." The same philosophy holds true for rooms.

Who Needs a Decorator or a Designer?

The answer to this question depends upon what changes the space or rooms require. Will it be a major job, such as fixing bad plaster and resurfacing floors, moving electrical outlets, or relocating walls? If the job involves a major overhaul, by all means consult a decorator or a designer. If the project entails building platforms, installing complicated lighting, or designing built-in cabinetry, a designer or decorator will certainly save you needless heartache. Conversely, if it is simply a question of choosing a color scheme and deciding upon a suitable furniture arrangement, most people feel that they can tackle the project themselves—especially if they have done the homework outlined in this book.

It never hurts to obtain the advice of experts—even if you don't end up hiring them. As was stated earlier, they earned their stripes through practical experience, having solved most of those "insurmountable" problems that every novice encounters for the first time. If your budget is sizable, say around $10,000, then by all means consult a professional, preferably several, before selecting one.

NOTES TO YOUNG MARRIEDS

Newlyweds are notorious for making the wrong decorating decisions. Their first purchases are invariably sources of regret at a later point in their lives. The problem is basically a lack of exposure to the full range of decorating options. Newlyweds tend to settle for department-store clichés or some mass manufacturer's poorly designed and overpriced line of furniture. It is like purchasing a cheap dress with a bad cut: it will never lay right; the hem will be uneven; the zipper will always bulge; it will simply never fit properly.

A department-store executive employed by a very famous New York-based firm confided to me the other day that people in the middle-income range have the hardest time getting any value for their hard-earned dollars. Those individuals with a lot of money can easily afford to purchase fine antiques which will not lose their value. People with very little money make do with what they find, generally settling for second-hand furniture and amusing pieces with low price tags. The real trap for people with moderate incomes lies in buying furniture that is too expensive for the purpose for which it is intended. These individuals permit their expectations to outstrip their knowledge. The furniture they finally select is invariably pretentious. The things we crave when we are young are a far cry from what we ultimately end up with as we grow older and our tastes become more sophisticated. Culture enriches us. It broadens our horizons. We become fuller, wiser, more knowledgeable human beings. Change is the most vibrant, the most painful, yet ultimately the most rewarding aspect of living. Newlyweds suffer from a certain naïveté.

So what are they to do? They are entering the most important phase of their lives—setting up a home that symbolizes their new status. Funds are usually tight. The first home is usually small, generally a rented apartment. Most newlyweds cannot afford to pay for the advice of a decorator and some might not have access to the ones with the best advice even if they could. Where do they start?

Rented spaces require a different decorating approach than that employed for a house which the family owns. Structural changes are generally not an option in rental situations, so most people leave the apartment as it is. They prefer to invest in furnishings and accessories that they can either take with them when they move or resell to recoup some of their investment.

Cosmetic or transportable decorating is the answer. Everything— bookshelves, paintings, floor coverings, furniture—has to be assessed on two levels. Is it cheap enough to abandon with no regrets when the lease is up, or is it expensive enough to have some resale value? (See the discussion of the two-year plan in the earlier portion of this chapter.) There are certain necessities without which no one can live comfortably: a table and four dining-room chairs; living room seating for four to six individuals; a good bed; a place to store books and records; and hi-fi equipment. Most couples who possess these items can lead a reasonably comfortable existence.

We are still dealing in rather abstract terms: a table, chairs, seating, storage. What will they look like? The first principle to remember is: don't get furniture that matches. Stay away from "coordinated" furniture, e.g., a matched bedroom set and sofa with two matching chairs. Think in terms of freshness, color, originality. Select furniture that is cheerful or bold. Select chairs for the kitchen or dining-room table that are brightly colored, e.g., bistro chairs or director's chairs. The latter come in a huge range of canvas colors and wood frames to harmonize with other things in the room. The director's chair is an unheralded classic of twentieth-century design. It looks great in the living room, at the dining-room table, in the den, or even out on the patio or terrace. But if this chair is too ubiquitous, there are several others which are almost as versatile: bentwood café chairs; ladderback chairs; stackable plastic chairs; natural wood chairs with rush seats— all are inexpensive and good looking.

Newlyweds should keep value in the forefront of their minds. Their options are much more varied than they suppose. The best sources for furniture are auctions, flea markets, barn sales, tag sales, and Goodwill Industries. These markets are still the best places for bargains. Besides, they are a whale of fun and make furniture shopping a pleasurable way to spend the afternoon.

Terrific interiors have been created from among things that others have discarded, furniture picked up right off the street (check out the best sections in town on bulk pick-up night), at the town dump, or at the junk yard. Upholstery is generally the most expensive item to purchase for the house or apartment. Victorian settees, fainting couches, and fringed ottomans dating back to grandmother's time can be made to look as glamorous as custom upholstery with a fresh application of paint and new slipcovers. All it takes is a little imagination and sweat equity.

Another way to save money on seating is by using pillows. These can be set on a raised plywood platform that's been carpeted to match the floor. Banquettes made up of loose seat and back pillows have a sleek, modern effect that gives a room a unified appearance. Designers usually make L-shaped units and dispense with individual chairs. Not having a roomful of chair legs makes the space seem larger.

Lighting, which has already been discussed in a separate chapter, might be mentioned again briefly here. Light, that magical space transformer, should be considered creatively wherever a budget is meager. Track lights are an excellent investment since they accept a variety of fixtures. Spots and wall washers, for example, can easily take the place of paintings; a warm pool of light on the fireplace wall is just as exciting as a painting. Similarly, a glow of light in a darkly painted hallway is almost all that's needed to decorate the space. Light cans placed on the floor or hidden in large plants send a spray of light up through the leaves to the ceiling, thus creating a highly decorative pattern. A single halo of light suspended over the dining-room table, over an object, or in one part of the room while the remainder lies in semidarkness can be both glamorous and exciting. Guests will really enjoy the atmosphere.

Plants produce fabulous results for rooms decorated on tight budgets. Hang lush plants from the tops of windows (forget curtains) and place tall ones in the corners of the room. Use them to fill in holes near tables or next to lamps. Keep them healthy and bushy by pinching them back all the time. Never, never use plastic plants. If insufficient light is a major problem, use baskets of dried flowers, dried grasses, dried hydrangeas, dried tree branches—anything at all as long as it's natural and organic. Plastic flowers look unreal and are deadly in any decorative scheme.

Color is an all-important factor in making do with small budgets. When it comes to painting your interior, color is the least expensive way to add a sense of dash to any scheme. Be bold rather than timid: limit the scheme to one color plus white and an accent or two. A scheme like that is a sure-fire thing. White neutralizes, relieves, and offsets the bold color. Here's a hypothetical scheme: use blue and white because it's so popular. Walls can be painted Bristol blue, with the moldings around doors, windows, trim, and baseboard painted white. The sofa can be covered in a blue-and-white print or stripe, or blue and white plus another color; it can also be covered in solid white, straw, or in a lighter shade of blue. Draperies can consist of a heavy white fabric, such as linen or sailcloth, on wooden rods painted white. The carpet should be a neutral shade, natural sisal or hemp (that is, a yellow-beige tone); or it could also be a blue-gray synthetic or wool. Small objects in the room, such as pillows, posters, ceramic vases, and ashtrays, should contain brilliant accent colors—yellow, orange, coral. Also add several green plants, natural textures in the form of baskets and terracotta pots, plus something with a touch of black.

This basic scheme will necessarily undergo some modification in a new building since there are no moldings or wood trim. But it should still work. In this case, treat one important wall (usually the one against which the sofa is placed) as a color plane. Paint it Bristol blue and leave the three remaining walls white. Again, the sofa can be covered in a blue-and-white print, a solid white or off-white sailcloth, or a blue-and-white stripe. The color scheme for the floor coverings should be repeated exactly as outlined earlier. Remember to repeat the Bristol blue of the wall again for emphasis, either in the form of throw pillows, as a printed skirt for a table, a throw rug, or as the upholstery on a side chair. Accents on tables should be the same as earlier.

Whatever scheme is finally selected, remember to use natural textures—hemp, terracotta planters, natural caning, wicker, sisal, baskets, and natural woods. These are leavening. They dispel the aura of coldness and stuffiness from any room and harmonize the interior. They can literally do no wrong—they improve, enhance, enliven, and invigorate your abode.

One Last Word

The most important thing to remember is not to take all this so seriously. Everyone responds more favorably to a personal and daring decorative scheme (even your boss) than one that's pretentious and obviously intended to look expensive. Decorating on a budget gives one a chance to experiment, to make a few natural mistakes. A garish print which is used to recover a secondhand sofa can turn out to be a smashing success—or at the very least something you're able to put up with for a year or two. However, if the same sofa covered in the identical print cost $700 brand new, it would clearly be a disaster.

Starting out as newlyweds represents a great opportunity to have some fun, to learn some basic principles about shopping and do-it-yourself techniques. Learning how to wield a paintbrush, refinish a cabinet, line the drawers of an old chest with bookbinder's paper so that you are pleasantly surprised each time the drawer is opened—that's the fun of decorating. This is truly a joyous time in both your lives. Relax and don't take things too seriously. The more experimenting you do now when funds are low, the better equipped you will be to make meaningful decisions on decorating when the chips roll in.

THE FOUR DECORATIVE MOVEMENTS

THE TRADITIONAL SCHEME

Rooms decorated in the traditional style bring together the patina of antique surfaces, the richness of pattern, texture, and color, the warmth of paintings and objects. To look through the interiors that follow, one can easily see why the traditional room retains such a strong appeal to so large an audience. The roots of the traditional interior lie in Europe in the eighteenth century, in the manor houses of England, the châteaux of France, and the palazzos of Italy. Of course, America has also contributed a tradition of grand interiors. Many people prefer the unpretentious grace of the American styles—Colonial, Chippendale, Federal, and Empire—to the grandeur of their European cousins and counterparts.

Despite the perennial popularity of the traditional interior, changes have been occurring in such decorative schemes. More and more, we are finding contemporary seating—sofas and easy chairs instead of rigid formal settees—because today's demand for comfort is stronger than ever. Color schemes, too, are richer and more vibrant. The rainbow pastels of jonquil yellow, melon, spring green, sky blue, to name just a few, are increasingly being used for wall colors and for upholstery even on fine antique chairs and settees. The bright colors freshen and enhance a room full of dark wood antiques and reproductions. Perhaps the greatest trend of all is the use of traditional furniture in a thoroughly modern setting and with modern art. All three are immeasurably enhanced by the juxtaposition, as you will see illustrated in this chapter.

Dark, lacquered walls provide a
dramatic setting for this collection of
modern and Oriental art in a
Manhattan living room.

PHOTO: BERNARD LIEBMAN

A SETTING OF elegance, individuality, and dramatic lighting distinguishes the dining room, *left*, of Mr. and Mrs. J. M. Kaplan in New York. The dark, glossy walls offset the couple's unique art works, which they have collected for many years. Behind the table is a woven sculpture of great visual power. Next to it is a polychromed Santos, displayed on a pedestal. Except for the art, the room is almost devoid of furnishings. There is an Empire table and eight dining chairs. The room's uncommon drama derives not only from the art but also from the lighting. The light sources are completely hidden by a ceiling cove and focused to accentuate the art.

The pine-paneled library, *right*, is lined with bookshelves displaying books and rare artifacts, such as the Cycladic head and small ancient gold and bronze sculptures in lucite cases. The recesses of the bookcases are painted a dark tone and lighted to show off the objects. Furnishings are an easy mix of contemporary sofas in red velvet. Small Jacobean footstools are both occasional tables and library steps. The modern chrome-base coffee table is underscored by the Oriental rug.

PHOTOS: BERNARD LIEBMAN

The living room combines art and furnishings from different stylistic periods and nations. Over the seating banquette, *left,* is a modern painting by Claudio Bravo and, next to it, a superb Japanese folding screen, which is hung like a painting. A Buddha is displayed dramatically against the dark walls over the fireplace. Furniture is an eclectic mix of contemporary seating, French Louis XV chairs and stools, and a Spanish table, that is set with a bowl of peonies, just off the entrance to the room. The dining room can be glimpsed through the open doorway.

The foyer, *vignette,* continues the dark color scheme. It is furnished with a French gilt console and mirror, flanked by English footstools and framed drawings.

Shuttered windows and walls covered in yellow silk fabric give the bedroom a warm ambiance. The pair of lounge chairs introduce the strong splash of red to the scheme. Over the marble mantel, an antique French mirror reflects the early American portrait painting on the opposite wall.

PHOTOS: BERNARD LIEBMAN

DESIGNER MARIO BUATTA's New York apartment has the richness of pattern and exotic furniture that is associated with the English Regency period. In the living room, *left*, the walls are glazed yellow, a color which sets off the blue-and-white porcelains. Although the sofa and lounge chairs are contemporary, most of the tables in the room are antiques of the Regency period. The cabriole-leg table between the windows is Portuguese. The rug repeats the room's blue-and-white color accent, and so do the chintz draperies at the windows.

A lacquered Queen Anne secretary brings a strong red accent into the yellow-and-blue scheme. Its red tone is repeated in the skirt covering the table in an adjacent corner.

The designer's collection of Delft and eighteenth-century Chinese export porcelains, the room's major accessories, are displayed on tabletops and on the wall shelves on either side of the fireplace, *lower right.*

PHOTOS: RICHARD CHAMPION

Red, the color of beaujolais, covers the walls of designer Mario Buatta's bedroom, *right*. The Regency four-poster bed has a tented canopy and curtains. The American patchwork quilt repeats the red-and-white scheme. Next to the window is a rare cabinet-on-stand, decorated with "pen-and-ink work," which was a handcraft done by ladies in the early nineteenth century much the way that women today do needlepoint. Over the cabinet is a bull's eye mirror and bracket displaying a porcelain vase.

A white-painted architectural bookcase faces the bed, *top left.* Its pedimental top is flanked by porcelain Fu dogs. A lacquered antique desk sits before the bookcases. In this vignette the intricacy of the pen-and-ink work can be clearly seen in the close-up of the cabinet door.

The bedside table, *left*, affords the designer with a place to arrange his collections into still lifes. White porcelain dogs stand behind a carved coral box. An eighteenth-century Chinese painting-on-glass hangs over a dressing mirror set in a bamboo frame.

PHOTOS: RICHARD CHAMPION

THIS LIVING ROOM of great elegance and restraint was designed by Anthony Hail of San Francisco. He used the family's portraits and rare Chinese treasures as the backbone of the scheme. The yellow walls are outlined with white moldings, *left*. A contemporary sofa, also in a yellow tone, blends unobtrusively into the room's background. The Oriental treasures are subtly incorporated into the scheme, the Chinese lacquered tables beside the sofa and the superb porcelains on the wall brackets. The rug is also from China.

Over the mantel, *right*, a carved wood swag frames an American portrait, thus combining the two disparate elements into an arresting focal point. The red of the man's jacket in the painting is echoed in the upholstery on a Louis XV armchair. Another Chinese rug defines this conversation group, which includes the sofa covered with a velvet leopard throw, Chinese side chair, and table.

The foyer is a repository of exquisite antique Chinese furniture—the console table and pair of armchairs and, beneath the table, a Chinese traveling chest. The pair of wall sconces in red lacquer chinoiserie flank a contemporary painting.

PHOTOS: JEREMIAH O. BRAGSTAD

LEE RADZIWILL believes in a dash of the unexpected, an element of surprise in decorating. Rather than stick to one period or style, she selects objects of good quality to create the common link for compatibility. In the Radziwill library, walls are covered in blue-grey fabric that merges into the tie-back draperies, also of the same fabric. The sofa is purposely big for seating three in comfort. It is covered in leopard-print velvet that is repeated on two x-base footstools. A collection of antique portraits is hung around the room in unusual starburst frames. The rug introduces the zest of another print, a geometric design in the same colors as the leopard print.

The Radziwill drawing room, *lower right,* is a splash of reds—the color of the walls and that used for most upholstery covers. The marble mantel is classical in its styling, topped by a marble and gilt mirror. Centered on the mantel is a fifth-century Roman head.

The dining room has both walls and windows sheathed in the same red moiré fabric. The tour de force of the room is the set of magnificent gilded Regency dining chairs. Note their unusual front legs, shaped like a lion's forelegs. The chairs surround a Regency pedestal dining table and also line the room. The painting over the French commode is another Regency whimsy, a "dog-and-monkey" painted by John Wooten.

PHOTOS: RICHARD CHAMPION

109

THE MANHATTAN living room, *right,* is at once stylishly chic and invitingly casual. The design firm, Parish-Hadley Inc., accomplished that duality by keeping the room's background very subtle (although there is a hint of marbelizing on the beige walls). The tall recessed bookcases also give the room a sense of order. Then comes the decorative panache of the herringbone-pattern parquet floors and the punch of the two zebra-striped batik pillows. The large contemporary sofa is covered in white linen; the chairs are Louis XV armchairs with painted frames. The tables in the room all share an Oriental exoticism: the black laquered lamp table, the Chinese-style coffee table, and the unusual inlaid console beside the window.

The bedroom has twin beds with painted frames and shirred muslin curtains. The blue color of the bedposts is repeated in the folding screen, which bears an Italian architectural mural. The melon tint of the walls was derived from the color of the drapery fabric.

The flying staircase displays a collection of nineteenth-century paintings of whimsical scenes and animals.

PHOTOS: TOM WIER

A COLOR SCHEME of white-on-white with a touch of red contributes to the vibrancy of the living room, *left*. It was designed by Joseph Braswell who positioned the magnificent Coromandel screen as the focal point for the room's major seating group. The screen is balanced by the unified drapery treatment on the adjoining wall. Contemporary sofas mix with Louis XV armchairs, tables, and footstools. Underscoring it all is the superb red-and-white area rug, featuring stylized flowers and geometric pattern.

The foyer, *top right*, is impressively sumptuous. It has an inlaid marble floor and is rimmed by marble columns. The ceiling is painted blue to look like a patch of sky, seen through a skylight.

Although the room is grand in scale, it has small, intimate areas for conversation, such as this one before the fireplace. A *trumeau* tops the marble mantel; between the French armchairs and the contemporary sofa is a red-lacquer Chinese table.

PHOTOS: NORMAN MCGRATH

The scheme of two colors is one of the most effective—and the easiest for the novice to handle. In the bedroom, *left,* the room is decorated in essentially two colors, the vibrant red of the walls and the oyster white of the carpet and window and bed draperies. The upholstery of the wing chair repeats the red wall color. The wood furniture in the room, such as the bed frame, the chest of drawers, and a small Pembroke table by the side of the wing chair, introduce the dark accent to the light scheme. Upholstery of a Victorian armchair adds another accent color, a dash of gold.

Another view, *right,* illustrates designer Joseph Braswell's adroit handling of such strong color. Rather than paint all four walls of the room in red, that tone stops at the fireplace wall. This wall is left white for visual relief. There are, however, small red accents, such as the background color of the painting and the wing chair upholstery.

A small room makes a compact study, *bottom left.* It is just wide enough for the desk and built-in bookcases. Framed prints line the adjacent wall, hung above the antique French commode and a French side chair.

PHOTOS: NORMAN MCGRATH

GEORGIAN STYLING never seems to be dated. It is as popular today as it has been for more than two centuries. The living room, *overleaf*, is a classic example of the Georgian blend of elegance and informality. The paneled walls and the denticulated molding at the ceiling gave designers Barbara Jaffe and Carol Ann Hayden the cue for the room's eighteenth-century English decoration. The grouping before the fireplace combines a camel-back settee with two Chippendale armchairs, all covered in a yellow damask fabric. In one corner of the room is a lacquered Queen Anne secretary decorated with chinoiserie; opposite it, a skirted table is flanked by two Hepplewhite armchairs. Most of the tables in the room are also eighteenth-century English antiques, except for the chrome-and-glass coffee table, which is a modern classic by Mies van der Rohe.

The contemporary wallpaper provides a modern touch in the foyer, *left*. The William and Mary chest is topped by a Georgian mirror and flanked by two side chairs with turned legs typical of the Elizabethan style.

The large, gilt Chinese Chippendale mirror, which tops an equally impressive black lacquered buffet, is the focal point of the dining room. Two different tables, a small one in front of the bay window, and a larger one in the room's center, create both formal and intimate places to dine. The tables are surrounded by a set of eight Queen Anne chairs with seats covered in a flamestitch pattern.

The dominant red color of the library is relieved by white—the painted bookcases, the marble mantel, and the ceiling. Textures also tone down the red scheme; there is a damask print covering the Chippendale armchair, a red flamestitch fabric on the tall, "landlord's" chair, and an assortment of colors and pattern in the Oriental rug. Except for the contemporary sofa and the coffee table, the occasional furniture in the room is predominantly eighteenth-century English in style.

PHOTOS: NORMAN McGRATH

DESIGNER HARRISON CULTRA'S country home, an historic Hudson River landmark where Robert Fulton once lived, has a superb simplicity about it. Although it is furnished with antiques, the ambiance is modern, which results from the spaciousness of the rooms and from the designer's controlled use of accessories. The dining room, *left*, epitomizes this ambiance. The Adam mantel is graced by a gilt mirror of nineteenth-century design. The window treatments, too, are subdued, simple swags of the vermilion silk. Two different styles of French chairs, pairs of Louis XV and Empire, are used around the French, 1930s folding dining table. The area rug is natural sisal.

The entrance hall, *top right*, is a double-height room with a stairwell, rimmed by a balustrade of Chinese Chippendale fretwork. A French *trumeau*, two urn-shaped lamps, and a stone sphynx rest on the foyer table. On the upstairs landing, the arched hallway to the bedrooms frames the windows, which are located directly over the entrance door.

The living room, *right*, is rimmed by floor-to-ceiling French doors, opening to the garden. Walls are painted a spring green to echo the plantings outside; that color is picked up on the low banquette in front of the fireplace and on several small French chairs. The rest of the seating is contemporary and covered in natural linen. A sisal area rug covers the dark-stained wood floors.

PHOTOS: NORMAN MCGRATH

The fabulous four-poster bed gives Harrison Cultra's bedroom an air of fantasy. The pagoda-shaped top is swagged and tented with a printed cotton fabric. An American patchwork quilt in the same colors, which the designer found in a relative's attic, is a fortunate match as the bedspread. Across the room, a large chaise longue makes a comfortable spot to read next to the fireplace. The two windows have colorful chintz draperies; between them is a red lacquered bureau and a Queen Anne mirror, both English antiques.

To offset the bed's boldness, the rest of the room's furnishings are restrained. There are two small tabouret tables and matching lamps on either side of the bed and, across from it, an antique American chest and mirror.

The downstairs sitting room, *right*, is a repository of Robert Fulton memorabilia and other lore of the region. The inventor of the steamboat was the son-in-law of the house's original builder, Hon. Walter Livingston. Old maps and prints of steamboats line the walls on either side of the fireplace. These can be seen in the vignette, *top right*. The blue chintz fabric, used to slipcover the two sofas, is seen again as a border for the draperies and valances. On the floor, a beautiful Oriental rug.

PHOTOS: NORMAN McGRATH

OLD WORLD ELEGANCE at its
height describes the Manhattan townhouse of designers
Robert Denning and Vincent Fourcade. The size and architecture of the
rooms is grand in scale, which the
designers dramatize with overscaled
furniture. One of the dining areas is
situated on the marble-tiled landing
of the stairwell, *right*. The dining
group consists of a marble-top pedestal table and three Louis XVI *fauteuils*, with red leather upholstery
that repeats the carpet color.
Beneath the bend in the staircase
there is just enough room for a
French commode.

The drawing room has walls covered
with a large-scale chintz fabric that
is also used to slipcover the sofa.
Between the windows is a red lacquered cabinet and, beside it, a
French desk. A French *marquise* and
footrest face the fireplace.

The bedroom, *left*, continues the
exaggerated scale in the Directoire
sleigh bed and wallpaper pattern,
which resembles Italian tilework.
Marble busts on wall brackets and
other statuettes are exotic decorative
touches. Over the fireplace is a lacquered Chinese mirror.

A tiny guest bedroom doesn't let its
size detract from its grandeur. So
close are the quarters that there is
only space for the canopy bed, hung
inside with a Venetian port scene,
and across from the bed, an eighteenth-century English architectural
bookcase.

PHOTOS: NORMAN MCGRATH

THE SUBTLETY OF the beige color scheme and the display of Oriental art contribute to this living room's serenity. It is the apartment of designer Anthony Hail in San Francisco. The marble fireplace and its French mirror, *left*, provided the room's natural focal point, which the designer enhanced with crystal light sconces and the panels of a Japanese screen on either side.

The room's ambiance is French, *top right*. There is a mix of Louis XV and XVI tables and chairs, several covered in leather, a French crystal chandelier, and two contemporary sofas. The *boiserie*, inset with bookcases, is painted in contrasting tones. The two conversational seating groups are tied together by the colorful Oriental carpet.

Chinese artifacts, which Tony Hail collects, are tastefully arranged on tabletops and on the mantel shelf, *vignette*. The French table with its raised gallery displays a collection of early Chinese pots; the lamp base is also a Chinese jar.

The windows, *right*, are floor-to-ceiling French doors, simply treated with beige velvet draperies. Between the windows is a French Empire desk and pair of leather-covered French *fauteuils*.

PHOTOS: JEREMIAH O. BRAGSTAD

The bathroom in the Hail apartment, *left*, has a masculine air, derived from the glossy dark wall color, the framed prints, and antique bathroom fixtures. A low leather bench faces the marble bathtub. The velvet draperies are the same wine color as the walls. In the window alcove is an antique dressing table.

The foyer, *top*, is also masculine in mood. Walls are painted in trompe l'oeil rustication to resemble blocks of stone. A pair of French chairs flank the marble-top console table, which is set with a bust of Napoleon.

The bedroom has walls covered with striped fabric, framed prints of architectural renderings, a French bedspread with a fur throw, and an Empire chest for the night table.

PHOTOS. JEREMIAH O. BRAGSTAD

WITH A MONOCHROMATIC color scheme of gold and white, designer Joseph Braswell created a living room of great sumptuousness in the French style. The room's white-painted *boiserie*, highlighted with gold leaf, is echoed in the color of the upholstered furniture. Before the fireplace are twin banquettes with white covers edged in gold fringe and strewn with large gold-tone pillows. The frame of a *fauteuil* is also gilt. On the floor is a magnificent antique Aubusson carpet, prized for its stylized flower pattern and pale color palette.

The French theme spills over into the dining room, *top right,* where a French oval dining table is surrounded by French-style chairs. Despite the dark brown walls, the ambiance of the room is bright and cheerful. The contradiction results from the relief afforded by large areas of white—the white painted wood trim, the white floor and ceiling.

The foyer has a *trumeau* over a console table, flanked by twin Louis XVI *fauteuils.* In the back of the hallway is an antique Coromandel screen. Lighting in the marble-tiled hall includes gilt sconces and a brass lantern.

PHOTOS: NORMAN McGRATH

Within a large and formal French drawing room, designer Joseph Braswell created several smaller areas for conversation, music, and game playing. The black concert grand piano, a black table lamp, and lacquered tea table are strong accents in the otherwise white-and-gold room; they provide a necessary contrast to all the lightness. Large potted palms also soften the room's formality.

The *boiserie* door panels conceal the bar located behind the bridge table, *top right*. It is seen with the doors open. The game table's mirrored top reflects the glitter of the bar shelves. The game chairs are in the Louis XV style.

Walls of the powder room are papered in a tailored stripe in traditional French Directoire colors: black and gold. Above the marble counter and gold basin are two tole lamps to light the mirror.

PHOTOS: NORMAN McGRATH

THE DECORATIVE SCHEME for this Manhattan penthouse was strongly influenced by that of a Georgian manor house. The pine paneling has typical Georgian details, such as the wall niches on either side of the fireplace, window treatments, and the ceiling cornice. Designers Denning and Fourcade selected rare English antiques to furnish the room. Over the mantel is a Chinese Chippendale mirror and next to the window is a baroque lacquered cabinet on a richly carved and gilded stand. A Regency library table backs the sofa; it has unusual gilt scrolls on the legs. A large ottoman with turned legs in four separate sections provides the room with extra seating.

An oversized sofa, *top right,* in a colorful chintz slipcover, is one of the several places to sit in the room. There are also banquettes in the far corners, one beneath the window and the English daybed beside a tapestry screen just off the entrance to the room. The tall Régence armoire, decorated with ormulu mounts, introduces a touch of French to the predominantly English scheme.

The dining room is far from formal despite its crystal chandelier, pine paneling, and antique Dutch portrait. The Queen Anne dining chairs are painted to resemble animal spots and the small piano sports a geometric pattern.

PHOTOS: NORMAN MCGRATH

WALLS LACQUERED the color of a rain forest turn this small room into an exceptionally cozy retreat. Designer Mario Buatta repeated the blue-and-white chintz on the windows as the draperies and on the sofa as a slipcover. A small Queen Anne secretary, decorated with chinoiserie, *top left*, introduces a flash of red for accent. It is used with an Italian painted armchair. The small child's chair adds a whimsical touch.

The room's diverse patterns; *bottom left*, vitalize the scheme: There is a green-and-white windowpane plaid as the table skirt, the chintz on the sofa, and the contemporary blue-and-white squiggle print on the Edwardian slipper chair. The rug, a needlepoint design with stylized tulips, repeats the dark green and white. Note how the Regency genre painting is hung from a ribboned bow.

The unusual placement of the fireplace, *right*, dictated the position of the sofa, on the opposite wall. Over the mantel is a gilt Regency mirror and, beside it, a nineteenth-century English lacquered cabinet.

PHOTOS: PETER REED

CERTAINLY THE MOST fortunate of decorative marriages occurs between sleek modern architecture and antique furniture. An example of this compatibility is the renovated New York townhouse of Robert Glenn Bernbaum. The interiors were modernized into the clean, open spaces shown here. The owner, with designer Albert Hadley, of Parish-Hadley Inc., planned the new interiors around a collection of English and French antiques.

In the dining room, *left*, the new spiral staircase rises like a piece of sculpture. Its sleek design complements the Louis XV armchairs and the round dining table. A French provincial cupboard and a low serving cabinet are the room's only other furniture. The contemporary rug in a stylized Navaho design was made in Portugal.

The living room, *top right*, brings together different stylistic periods—but the contemporary upholstered seating in beige linen acts as the decorative leaven for the mix. Most of the tables are French; the mirror over the mantel is a gilt Régence antique; the footstool is Italian. Two French *bergères* are covered in black leather. Because the color and pattern in the room is so controlled, the room can take the boldly patterned and colored Portuguese rug.

Another view of the dining room, *right*, focuses on the window wall overlooking the private garden and its lighted fountain. Over the fireplace is a portrait of the owner's mother.

PHOTOS: NORMAN MCGRATH

The bedroom, *top left,* is furnished
as if it were a sitting room. The daybed is upholstered in leather and
spread with a fur throw and batik
pillows. An eighteenth-century Queen
Anne secretary is finished in black
lacquer with rich chinoiserie decoration. The occasional table and lamps
are contemporary; the side chair is
a French antique.

The adjoining dressing room, *bottom
left,* has a mirrored wall reflecting
the closet doors. A French provincial
table is used for depositing jewelry
and emptying pockets in the evening.
The doorway looks into the sumptuous bathroom, which even has its
own fireplace.

The staircase, *right,* continues as a
sculptural spine through three levels
of the townhouse. It leads from the
downstairs dining room into the
living room on the second level. The
blue-painted study can be glimpsed
through the doorway. What could
have been wasted space, the area between the two rooms next to the staircase, is furnished with a folding tray
that serves as the bar.

PHOTOS: NORMAN McGRATH

Nothing is more deadly to the traditional decorating scheme than flat, dull colors. It is a common mistake made by many people decorating a traditional room. Antique furnishings and reproductions are greatly enhanced by the use of bright pastels. Designer David Whitcomb illustrates the effect in this house in Connecticut, distinguished by its architectural details. In the entrance hall, *top left,* is a handsome flying staircase and a Palladian window.

The living room, *top right,* takes its color scheme of jonquil yellow walls and white wood trim, the rose-tone draperies and upholstery covers from the area rug, which is a rainbow of twenty-six colors. The furniture is an eclectic mix of two Georgian armchairs by the fireplace and a pair of painted Empire side chairs grouped around a French *gueridon* in front of the window.

The master bedroom is comfortably furnished as a small sitting room with a contemporary chaise longue and lounge chair on either side of the fireplace. A skirted table and two Empire chairs furnish the area in front of the bay window. The juxtaposition of an antique oval painting and the large modern painting of seashells is a pleasing contrast.

The garden room, *right,* resembles a trellissed loggia because of the designer's use of latticework and shutters. The green-and-white color scheme was taken from nature and introduces accents of red on the sofa and two folding chairs for spice.

PHOTOS: ROBERT PERRON

PLUMP, CONTEMPORARY SOFAS and tree-size plants have removed much of the stiff formality from eighteenth-century French styling. In this Manhattan living room the *boiserie* lining the room was the starting point for the French scheme. Designer Harriet Epstein chose a variety of French chairs, some Louis XV and others Louis XVI, to blend with the large sofa. This room also had a magnificent view of Central Park so the designer raised the floor one step up near the window and installed the new window wall to capitalize on that view. Trees in pots turn this area into a greenhhouse.

The opposite side of the living room, *bottom right*, shows another conversation area with a grouping of a French settee and side chairs, an antique lacquered bureau-on-stand, and a glimpse into the foyer. The rug is an antique Savonnerie.

A canopy bed dominates the master bedroom, *left*. The frame and four posts are carved of wood to look like gnarled vines. A child's daybed, covered in patchwork fabric, serves as a bench at the bed's foot. The floral wallpaper and carpet of ribboned bows give the room the mood of a garden pavilion.

PHOTOS: JAMES MATHEWS

145

A SPECTACULAR CARVED and polychromed baroque bed adds a magical touch to this California bedroom. The room's treasures were arranged by designer Jay Steffy. In the corner is a fine antique Japanese screen and, on the other side of the bed, an antique painting. The bedside tables are unpretentious Provincial-style designs, topped with tole lamps and Chinese porcelain jars.

An exotic painting and pair of rare Directoire chairs, *right*, are the ingredients of a fantasy setting. The chairs are remarkable for their rich carving and gilding. Winged sphynx appear at the juncture of the arm and seat and the foot details are also gilded. The black piano serves as a link between the chairs and the bizarre painting of feasting lions.

PHOTOS: JAY STEFFY

NO LONGER NECESSARY to keep out the drafts in medieval rooms, the canopy bed remains immensely popular today. Designer David Hicks of London has a very special way with the canopy bed as the two shown here point up. The bed draped in white fabric, *left*, is the room's central focal point. The rest of the furnishings, the bedside tables, two lamps, and the tubular metal folding chair are modern in design.

Across the room, *bottom left*, a French chaise longue and imposing French *armoire* are foils for other modern pieces—the parson's desk and the miror-sheathed treatment of the fireplace mantel. The monotone scheme makes the bedroom open and breezy in feeling.

In another bedroom setting, David Hicks used the awkward space between two doors to position the canopy bed. To offset the angularity of the wall and doors, the bed has a round canopy, turning the room's liability into a decorative asset.

Two French *bergères* create a seating area before the fireplace, *bottom right*, opposite the bed. The white walls provide a cool background for the accent colors, pale orange and mauve, picked out from the painting over the fireplace.

PHOTOS: NORMAN McGRATH

AMERICA ADOPTED the four-poster bed as its own; both historic preservations and landmark houses always include an example. The bedroom, *left*, is a superb plantation mansion called "Rattle and Snap" outside Nashville, Tennessee. The room's furnishings are fine American antiques such as the Sheraton bed, the oval-back Hepplewhite open armchair, and, situated in front of the fireplace, a Chippendale footstool, wingback chair, and American shaving stand.

Shirred fabric lines the walls of the bedroom, *above right*, and frames the Federal mantel. American silhouettes are hung on top of the shirring. The four poster has a shirred skirt, with coverlet and pillow shams embroidered in chinoiserie.

The bedroom in the attic of a restored Pennsylvania tenant's cottage, *above*, houses a fine colection of eighteenth-century American antiques. Owner Herbert Schiffer, an antiques dealer, installed the tester bed with a fish-net canopy, the ladderback chairs, and inlaid dower's chest in the room. The nineteenth-century appliqué quilt has a rare eagle motif.

Another bedroom in the Schiffer house, *right*, has an American pencil-post bed draped in gold colored homespun. It is spread with an Early American wool coverlet. The wing chair beside it wears a flamestitch cover made of needlepoint.

PHOTOS: LEFT, PETER REED,
RIGHT, NORMAN MCGRATH

A TROMPE L'OEIL MURAL of fruits and vegetables enlivens a California kitchen, *top left,* designed by Jay Steffy. Mexican quarry tiles surface both the backsplash and counter tops. The cabinets below the range are also painted to resemble rusticated stone.

A wallpaper, patterned after Italian tiles, *bottom left,* updates the kitchen in an older Manhattan apartment building. Rather than tear out the existing glass-door cabinets, designer Burt Wayne painted them a rich brown tone. He designed the center work island for additional storage space and work surfaces. Above the island, a butcher's rack holds pots and pans. Note that the old appliances were also integrated successfully into the new kitchen scheme.

Designers Jay Hyde Crawford and Anthony Tortora used the exposed brick wall as a departure point for the rustic setting of their Manhattan kitchen, *top right.* It is located in a landmark building. Other country touches are the patchwork fabric covering the dining table, farmhouse pots, accessories, and paintings.

The rustic wood cabinets and black-and-white checkerboard tile floors provide a suitable background for a collection of antique blue-and-white porcelains. The kitchen is situated in a 200-year-old tenant's cottage in Pennsylvania, owned and decorated by Mr. and Mrs. Herbert Schiffer. The room also has its original fireplace and pine mantel.

PHOTOS: TOP LEFT, JAY STEFFY; BOTTOM LEFT, PETER REED; TOP RIGHT, PAUL VANEYRE; BOTTOM LEFT, NORMAN MCGRATH

UPDATED TRADITIONAL

THE MOVE toward greater freedom in the mixing of modern and antique furniture and reproductions has been occurring with more frequency lately. The bolder and more daring the mix, the more updated is the traditional interior. This new direction in interior design carries with it a reminder of the past with a look toward tomorrow. It enjoys the best of both worlds, the past and the present.

In these rooms, we still see the use of many antiques and reproductions—paintings, furniture, accessories, lamps—but they are increasingly used as accents in a modern setting rather than as the predominant style. The modern flavor has become more and more important in these schemes while the antique furniture provides a wonderful cachet. Fine antiques are treated like art works, which is precisely what they are, treasures to be seen and enjoyed as objects. It is not necessary to fill a room to the rafters with everything derived from a single period, nation, or decorative style.

The updated traditional room still retains the warmth of the old world about it. But modern seating has replaced all but the occasionally used side chairs. The traditional interior is simply moving along with today's modern lifestyles and adapting to contemporary ways and needs. One could describe the new look in still another way—it's modern design without any of the hard edges.

Designer John Dickinson creates an interior of great originality in his own home, a converted firehouse in San Francisco. More of this unusual house follows on the next pages.

PHOTO: JEREMIAH O. BRAGSTAD

THERE IS an inventive streak about designer John Dickinson and the way he plans an interior. He is never afraid of drama or too timid to exaggerate scale. The living room of his firehouse, *left*, illustrates this theatrical flair. Using the windows as frames, he introduces two colossal heads on tall pedestals (which also incorporate the sound speakers). The unusual six-footed coffee table is another of his designs. The leather-covered sofa and lounge chairs are purposely low to contrast the scale of the pedestal figures.

Mr. Dickinson's love of the unusual shows in this detail, *top right*. It is a grouping of coral and other things from nature, eggs, baskets, and objects of his own design.

The full ambiance of the room is captured in this overall view, *bottom right*. Two settees and a complement of leather club chairs are grouped around the brass and stainless-steel fireplace. The wall and ceiling treatment is a trompe l'oeil effect to simulate the patina of ancient walls of crumbling buildings.

PHOTOS: JEREMIAH O. BRAGSTAD

More of designer John Dickinson's fantasy overflows into the dining area, *left*, where Victorian side chairs are lined up against the wall. The skylight plays up the unusual quality of the trompe l'oeil walls by shedding a beam of light over their rich surface. The dining table is a rare Art Nouveau design. Against the wall is a Dickinson-designed console table topped by porcelain jars.

The architectural model, *top right*, is actually the carved wood doors of Mr. Dickinson's clothes closet. It resembles nothing more than a typical Victorian streetscape of San Francisco in miniature.

Even the kitchen receives special treatment, *bottom right*. The sink is graced by a mirror made of plaster twigs. The pegs are used as a catchall for kitchen utensils.

A small vignette, *above*, reveals the designer's ability to find beauty in the simplest of forms. Here, a small white ironstone bowl and jars form an arresting still life on a side table.

PHOTOS: JEREMIAH O. BRAGSTAD

The master bathroom is dominated by the mirror and bathtub, both of which are highly unusual antiques. The bathtub, *right,* is rimmed in wainscot paneling that echoes the wood paneling of the room itself. The tub is also fitted out with antique brass faucets, handrails, and soap dishes. Twin drum tables on either side of it hold black porcelain ginger jar lamps with white shades. A marble-top washstand can be glimpsed in the foreground.

The bedroom, *left,* is furnished with *fau bambou* furniture, a Victorian marble-top bureau, and a small American Empire side chair covered in black leather. Note the unusual window treatment, a Roman shade, a typical Dickinson flourish.

PHOTOS: JEREMIAH O. BRAGSTAD

WITHIN THE SPACES of an 1880s Brooklyn brownstone building, designers Easton– La Rocca created a new modern setting for Mr. and Mrs. Stanley Cooper. The designers salvaged much of the old Victorian woodwork to use in the new scheme. In the library at the back of the house, *right*, the moldings were "stretched" or extended with the addition of new pieces to create the large pier glass behind the sofa. Across the room (not shown) they frame a new bookcase wall.

Four rental units were purged to form the spacious new living room, *left*, which shares its space with the dining room. The winding staircase is also new and leads up to the bedroom level. Its form is an attempt to get away from the ubiquitous spiral staircase. The doorway of the dining area is also new although the Victorian moldings give it an authentic flavor.

In the living room, *below left*, the gleaming walls, lacquered off-white, and the white upholstery make a pleasing but neutral background for the vibrant David Milne painting over the sofa and the accent of the Moroccan rug.

PHOTOS: DAVID EASTON

IN HIS NEW YORK townhouse, designer David Whitcomb brought together a melange of styles to create a scheme of great freedom and originality. Unifying the diverse elements, some modern pieces and some antiques, is the designer's sense of scale and his way with color. The living room, *far left,* has a window wall overlooking the garden that is covered with thin Venetian blinds flanking a yellow drapery panel. This acts as a backdrop for the florid English console table.

The contemporary cocktail table and sofa are foils for period accents, such as the English eighteenth-century armchair, covered in a flamestitch fabric, and the ten-part folding screen, papered in a Zuber mural. The screen shields the hallway to the front bedroom from view of the living room.

The bottom of the stairwell landing, *vignette middle,* holds a still life of two glazed terracotta figures, architectural ornaments salvaged from a nineteenth-century French building. On the upper landing, *vignette bottom,* a tall pedestal displays a Greek amphora.

The dining room, *left,* has a table surrounded by Regency side chairs. The room also overlooks a garden view (not shown).

PHOTOS: DANIEL EIFERT

The bedroom, *left,* with its desk, occasional chairs, and wall of books is both a library and study. The yellow walls are framed by dark moldings around the ceiling and windows, acting as outlines for the draperies. The tall Mithraic sculpture stands on one side of the bed.

The Parsons table-desk, *vignette,* is surfaced in an all-over patterned paper and displays the designer's collection of obelisks.

Tall bookcases, *top right,* line one entire wall and are painted black to contrast with the yellow walls. The back wall holds an antique chest and is hung with both modern and antique paintings.

The bedside grouping, *right,* affords another detailed look at the successful mix of different styles of art and accessories in the room.

PHOTOS: DANIEL EIFERT

THE TOWNHOUSE designed by David Easton and Michael La Rocca typifies the new direction that the traditional scheme has taken. This sophisticated setting results from surprisingly few elements, orchestrated by the lighting. The modern sofa, *right*, backed by a mirrored wall, is flanked by two black and gilt Regency armchairs. Windows are covered with simple, white drawstring Roman shades. The floors are carpeted in sisal matting. A statue of the double-faced Janus is the room's only art work. Light accents the scheme: uplights throw a spray of shadows from the plant foliage onto the ceiling while a spotlight dramatizes the sculpture.

The small sitting room, *left*, continues the living room's monochromatic color scheme, the mirrors, and the dramatic lighting. The daybed is a comfortable relaxing spot, flanked by two tables and a lamp. The mirrored panel modernizes the turn-of-the-century fireplace mantel.

The vignette, *top left*, picks up a view of the living room in a mirrored reflection over the fireplace mantel. In contrast to the light-toned walls in the rest of the apartment, the sleeping alcove is dramatically dark in wall tone and outlined by white moldings. The bed is covered with a white fur spread.

PHOTOS: RICHARD CHAMPION

ONE OF THE PRETTIEST gardens in New York belongs to designer Angelo Donghia. It opens from the ground-floor sitting room of his townhouse. He covered over the raised porch area with *trelliage,* creating a garden bower. On either side, there are built-in banquettes in a black and white awning-stripe fabric. (The black and white scheme continues indoors, too, seen through the open doorway.)

Mr. Donghia's living room, *top right,* has walls glazed a luminescent emerald green tone, which is made all the more dramatic by the contrast of white-painted formal architectural details: the pedimental moldings of the doorway and the crown cornice. Banquettes and slipper chairs are covered in white satin fabric. The ceilings and floors are also distinctively treated; the ceiling is papered with a silver leaf wallcovering and the floors are bleached to the color of sand.

The bedroom, *right,* uses only two colors, gray and white. Gray wool suiting fabric is used on the walls and for the bed and banquette upholstery. The white of the quilted draperies, over the roll-up bamboo blinds at the windows, is repeated in throw pillows and on the quilted bedspread.

PHOTOS: JAIME ARDELICE

DESIGNERS JAY HYDE CRAWFORD and Anthony Tortora relied on small-scale print fabrics and several spectacular objects to update a Manhattan brownstone built in the 1860s. In the living room, *far left*, slate gray walls and white moldings focus attention on the room's choice furniture accents, such as the eighteenth-century English console table. It is framed in a mirrored arch, reflecting the room's crystal chandelier. On the console table is a rare *blanc de chien* porcelain figure.

Other Oriental accents are used throughout the room, *vignette top left*. The fretwork table, covered in silverleaf, is topped by a yellow porcelain vase decorated with green dragons.

Sofa and chairs, *bottom*, are contemporary and wear a small print in a squiggle design. The painting over the sofa is by Claudio Bravo. In a corner, blue-and-white porcelain vases create a rich still life atop the black-lacquered Korean tea table. The coffee table is a slab of white-lacquered wood.

Silver and white geometric wallpaper animates the walls of the upstairs bedroom, where the platform bed is covered with two antique American patchwork quilts. A Victorian rope stool and a Venetian desk-table, modern painting, and African sculpture show the designers' flair for juxtaposition.

A guest bedroom, *above*, is just large enough for a single bed. It derives its charm from the fern wallpaper that is used as fabric for the Austrian shades in a reverse of the background and leaf colors.

PHOTOS: PAUL VANEYRE

173

ANTIQUE ACCESSORIES and pre-Columbian artifacts in this Manhattan living room reflect the owner's interest in art and design. Carl Levine, a department store executive, wanted the living room to recall the stucco-walled, white-beamed cottages of the south of France. The room's stucco-textured walls are a perfect foil for a mix of things rustic and polished—a sculptural steel chair by French artist Pergay, for instance, used with the terracotta figures. Mr. Levine's collection of pre-Columbian art forms striking vignettes throughout the room, *right*, filling the mirrored shelves in the wall niches on either side of the sofa and also the tops of tables.

Twin modern sofas, *top right*, are covered in a nubby Haitian cotton, which enlarges on the scheme's natural accents, such as the fur rug and velvet and fur throw pillows.

In contrast to the living room's light walls, those of the bedroom, *bottom right*, are dark and moody. Walls are covered in a men's wear worsted fabric and the bed has a leather spread. A collection of antique paintings lines the wall across from the bed.

PHOTOS: TOM WIER

THE COLOR SCHEME of pearl gray walls and off-white upholstery mingled with beige and chamois for accent reflects the trend toward subtle use of color. The furnishings of this Manhattan apartment, the home of designer Richard Neas, is a blend of period and modern. The antique chandelier, the Louis XV desk, and Provincial occasional table continue the French flavor provided by the two white-painted armoires, flanking the daybed, *left*. The slipper chair, covered in suede, and the Lucite coffee table are contemporary highlights.

The room's most outstanding feature is the painted floor, *right*, executed by owner Richard Neas, a trompe l'oeil artist. The design features large squares simulating the striation of cut agate. Another trompe l'oeil artistry is the treillage of the ceiling cove.

PHOTOS: NORMAN MCGRATH

IN A MONOCHROMATIC scheme of
great sophistication, designers
Mica Ertegun and Chessy Rayner
of Mac II, painted the walls of this
Fifth Avenue apartment a high-shine
charcoal brown. Everything else in
the room—the low-pile velvet carpet,
the three large contemporary sofas
and chairs, the window draperies—
is a crisp white. English antique side
tables blend with two modern parsons
tables, which are covered in a tortoise
shell finish, and with the two Chinese-
style coffee tables. For accent, there
are two English Chippendale
armchairs, with their seats covered
in a subtle brown-and-white polka
dot print.

The den, *above*, uses similar colors
but introduces more patterned
fabrics. The seating banquettes sport
a brown-and-white batik covering
and the walls are sheathed in a
brown-and-white diagonal stripe
fabric.

PHOTOS: NORMAN McGRATH

To ILLUSTRATE how well furniture and art can be resettled in new surroundings, compare this apartment of designer David Whitcomb with the townhouse, pages 164–167. Many of the same elements appear in both places because the designer moved them from his old townhouse into this new Beekman Place apartment. Mr. Whitcomb did not crowd the space with furniture but allowed the spatial quality to frame and offset his antiques and art. In the foyer, *top left,* one large modern painting fills the side wall. Next to it, a Greek vase rests on a severely simple pedestal beside the eighteenth-century English side chair. The bedroom can be seen through the doorway.

Mirrored ceiling panels inset between beams dramatize the bedroom, *bottom left,* reflecting the large antique painting. Another mirrored panel, beside the bed, creates the illusion that the room goes on and on.

The living room, *right,* combines a modern seating banquette, loveseat, and two small upholstered footstools with an antique English armchair. The room's airy quality results partly from the floors, which are bleached off-white in tone.

The dining area, *vignette,* is a simple setting of a red lacquered parsons table and two sculptural steel chairs.

PHOTOS: DANIEL EIFERT

THE BROWN-AND-WHITE color scheme has proved to be a popular combination in both modern and traditional interiors. Here, designer Tom Morrow uses it not only as the background of his urban townhouse, a Manhattan landmark, but also on nearly all of the room's upholstery. In the living room, *top right,* the brown-painted walls are outlined with crisp white moldings. The fireplace, typically Victorian in flavor, is accented by the gilt mirror over the mantel and by twin garden seats, topped by white shells.

In another view of the living room looking through the doorway to the back parlor, *bottom left,* a French side chair has a white-painted frame and leather seat and back cushions. A Victorian couch continues the brown scheme and adds the dash of a print throw pillow. Furniture in the back parlor is covered in brown-and-white printed slipcovers.

Baskets, antique lamps, paintings, and porcelains fill the room with charming still lifes, vignettes, *left.*

A printed wallpaper and matching bedspread, *bottom right,* give the guest bedroom a turn-of-the-century ambiance. An antique bamboo armoire on one wall balances the French daybed.

PHOTOS: RICHARD CHAMPION

183

RATTAN AND WICKER have moved indoors to give contemporary interiors a year-round feeling of summer. Designer Robert Perkins paired wicker pieces, such as the folding beach chair, round cocktail table, and small chair-side tables, with a sofa and slipper chair covered in an awning-stripe fabric. The huge plant and piles of pillows continue the garden mood in this city apartment of publicist Kecia Keeble. Floors are covered in natural sisal carpeting. The lacquered Chinese table and chest, seen in the foreground, hold *sang de boeuf* vases of fresh greenery.

For all its opulence, the apartment is only a small studio. Across the room, *right*, the bed is disguised as a sofa. It, too, is piled with pillows. Bookshelves on either side provide storage space for books and art objects. The doorway into the room is draped to echo the window treatment.

PHOTOS: NORMAN MCGRATH

A COLOR SCHEME of blue-and-white is an appropriate palette for a house in the country, *top right*. Designer Anthony Tortora chose a modern printed fabric to slip-cover the sofa (with its ruffled fringe), the lounge chair, and an ottoman. The wide plank floors and overhead beams suggested the rustic accents, such as straw stools for occasional tables, baskets, and the rag rug runner.

An old-fashioned settee, *top left*, was painted white and used with French garden chairs to continue the blue-and-white scheme out on the brick-paved patio. Together, they create a cool spot for summertime dining *al fresco*.

In the living room, *bottom left*, the owner's collection of blue-and-white porcelains create a delightful grouping with natural accents, such as the seashell and sunflowers. The still life rests on the console table behind a modern painting by owner Tortora.

In the bedroom, the all-white upholstered bed is set against a folding rattan screen, which forms the headboard. The room blends Chinese accents with French: the lacquered table and rug are Chinese in inspiration while the side chairs are mostly French designs.

PHOTOS: RICHARD CHAMPION

THE SOUTHWEST architecture of this house became the starting point for its superb Mediterranean mood. Designer Jay Steffy played up the tropical theme with shutters at the windows and rattan occasional chairs. The white sofa is offset by the large modern canvas. A mirrored panel next to the white-painted brick fireplace reflects the beamed ceiling and becomes the backdrop for an antique lacquered Chinese chest-on-stand.

The flying staircase and arched doorway in the foyer, *top right*, provides the excitement of curves. The doorway looks into the dining room where chairs are slipcovered to the floor. A wall shelf serves as the foyer table and is enhanced by the large mirror and overscaled garden urns.

Another view of the living room, *bottom right*, shows the seating banquette built into the corner. It is topped by a Ron Davis painting.

PHOTOS: PETER REED

THERE HAS BEEN a shift from insistent pattern toward the use of small, sophisticated prints. Designer Kevin McNamara first covered the walls of his Manhattan sitting room in a glossy tortoise shell vinyl. Then, he covered the corner banquette in a cotton fabric with a small-scale pattern. Pillows introduce a dotted white linen for contrast. There is a harmonious blend of natural accents, such as the tortoise shell bamboo blinds at the windows and the sisal carpeting on the floors.

Across the room, *right,* an antique Louis XVI desk is placed in front of the windows. Twin Louis XV armchairs are covered in shiny leather. Notice, though, that on the back, they sport another quiet plaid fabric (in foreground, left).

PHOTOS: NORMAN MCGRATH

A PERSONAL MIX of country antiques and contemporary art appears in this cooperative apartment in Manhattan. It is the residence of author Mary Ann Crenshaw, designed by William Machado.

In the foyer, *top left*, a contemporary wallpaper in a blue-and-white print is crisply outlined by the white moldings. The ceiling is painted a shade of blue. Displayed on the walls over a Mexican chest and a small country corner table are framed prints, drawings, baskets, and mirrors.

The owner collects both naive paintings and American quilts, several of which are displayed in the bedroom, *bottom left*. A fine American appliqué quilt with a schoolhouse design hangs on the bedroom wall. Another quilt covers the bed. The walls are upholstered in a blue-and-white cotton gingham. To the right of the framed quilt is a painting by Sister Gertrude of New Orleans.

In the living room, *top right*, an architectural bookcase and modern table-desk contrast with the antique country cupboard, which still wears its original red buttermilk paint. The eighteenth-century pine drop-leaf dining table is surrounded by American mule ear chairs.

The fireplace view, *bottom right*, illustrates the successful mix of contemporary seating—the rattan chairs and sofa, which is covered with a blue-and-white checked cotton—and antiques. An American pie safe sits beside the fireplace. White ceilings, moldings, and window shutters frame the yellow-painted walls.

PHOTOS: ROBERT PERRON

A FOUR-POSTER bed made of twined vines and draped in gauzy monk's cloth contributes to this bedroom's mood of quiet elegance. The monk's cloth is repeated as draperies over the door leading out to the terrace. A desk on a trestle base, used with an antique Italian footstool, echoes the simple lines of the bedside table. A fur throw, tossed over a lounge chair, is a touch of luxury.

The bedroom, *top right,* doubles as a retreat and quiet sitting area. The walls are draped in chocolate brown fabric as a foil for the modern painting and white upholstery. The chairs and ottomans are covered in the same white fabric as the bedcoverings. They create a conversation area around the fireplace. Designer Billy Gaylord introduced a crystal chandelier overhead and tropical plants to give this California bedroom a note of exotica.

PHOTOS: *left,* LO STUDIO; *right,* HORST

Kitchen design has been moving toward a country mood. The use of such natural elements as wood, brick, baskets, earthenware pots, and plants are the keynotes of the new direction. Designers Hermine Mariaux and Peter Neal used a ceiling of wood slats laid on the diagonal and a central cooking island to transport this kitchen miles away in mood from its Manhattan location. Birch wood cabinets, butcher block counters, vinyl tiled floors, and shuttered windows all contribute to the country flavor. In the corner, a seating banquette wraps around the saw-buck table, with rattan armchairs for pull-up seats.

A mosaic of brick spanning the walls and arching up the ceiling gives this Italian kitchen a rustic ambiance. An antique shelf and old, carved wood doors are inset into the brick work. The dining table is a single slab of well-worn wood and the chairs are rush-seat peasant farm furniture.

PHOTOS: LEFT, JAMES MATHEWS, RIGHT, EMMETT BRIGHT

EUROPEAN DESIGN

EUROPEAN INTERIORS exude personality. Each is different. Each attempts to be an original. On the Continent, the personal touch is prized more highly than adherence to the latest fashionable decorating trend. Perhaps it is because Europe grew up around kings, courts, and fine manor houses that, today, Europeans have a sure sense about what constitutes the good and successful interior. Style trends often begin here because of this bold attitude and desire for adventure. Europeans enjoy discovering new ways of putting things together decoratively.

There is also less need on the part of Europeans to prove their "good taste." Their ideal interior is a very personal environment where the inhabitant is surrounded by the furnishings and objects which he or she has selected and truly cares about—regardless of whether they all match or even share an affinity of style or design. To copy a trend is considered showy and only the nouveau riche would attempt to do it.

Italy ranks a special note. The interior design and architectural profession there is on the threshold of breakthroughs in the living environment. Although many Italians still prefer to live in their old palazzos, one soon discovers that the old buildings harbor stark, modern living arrangements. Italian architects and designers are among the most creative in the world and are continually creating new ideas and new trends.

A wonderful mix of period and modern furnishings and a fresh color palette contribute to this living room's personality. Here, there are no clichés, just a very individual mix. The neutral background of light beige sets the stage for color. The brightest tones come from the painting over the fireplace. The twin sofas pick up a tint of rose from the painting, while a Louis XV bergère adds a deeper rose. The residence was designed by David Hicks.

PHOTOS: LO STUDIO

THE TWO-STORY ENTRY hall of a fine British manor house, *top right,* is patterned with a blue-and-white paper with a Chinese theme. It rises up the stairwell walls through two levels. Moldings and balustrades are painted white to offset the paper's bold design. On the entry level, *right,* the paper provides the background for the florid baroque console table.

In one of the bedrooms, *top left,* the recessed niche displays a collection of blue-and-white porcelains. The wallpaper is a variation on the porcelain pattern. At the line of the moldings, the paper is bordered by a thin red stripe.

Another bedroom, *lower left,* is decorated in a fresh, green-and-white scheme, which is offset by a touch of turquoise fabric on the dressing table and chair. Old family portraits line the walls. Another view of this bedroom, *lower right,* shows the fireplace corner and a chaise longue.

The mantel of one of the house's many unusual fireplaces displays a collection of Royal Crown Derby china, *far right.*

PHOTOS: LO STUDIO

A 150-YEAR-OLD former coach house became this delightful country cottage in the south of France. Philip Wilson who manages Sotheby's of London uses it as a vacation house. The renovation was done by his brother, architect Tom Wilson. The living room, *left,* was made from two smaller rooms and a stairwell. The architect designed the new masonry fireplace to look as though it had always been there. He also designed the two sofas; they have wide backs and arms, large enough so people can perch on them during parties.

In the dining room, *vignette,* a wall niche with open shelves displays dishes which have a traditional blue-and-white pattern.

The kitchen, *top right,* although completely renovated, retains the charm of an old French farmhouse with its open shelves, tile floors, and slate work surfaces. Curves of the plaster-work and the rustic cooking utensils are in keeping with the mood.

The bathroom, *lower right,* is surfaced with colorful tiles set in a checkerboard pattern of alternating ochre and plum tones. They continue up the walls and across the arched ceiling.

PHOTOS: TIM STREET-PORTER

ODERN with a touch of whimsy describes this residence in Rome, the home of fashion designer Valentino, designed for him by Stefano Mantovani. The room was blessed with the vaulted brickwork ceiling, which the designer softened with a coat of white paint. To create a division between the foyer and the living room without cutting off the view of the arched ceiling, Mantovani designed the bamboo trellis work folding screen.

A series of trompe l'oeil trees are distributed around the room, *left*. Their tops are made from the same printed fabric that is used to cover the throw pillows and the sofa. A white ledge that steps down into the living room from the foyer is fitted with cushions to form a banquette for extra seating during parties.

The brilliant palette of the kilim rug, *right*, infuses the foyer with color. Twin lacquered Chinese console tables and bamboo-backed side chairs furnish the room.

PHOTOS: EMMETT BRIGHT

THIS SERENE SETTING in an older building in Italy illustrates the direction that interior design is taking. Furniture and architecture are merging to form the total environment. This apartment had superb vaulted ceilings as strong architectural features. The architects who planned the space, Giancarlo and Luigi Bicocchi and Roberto Monsani, designed the wall of lighted storage cabinets, arranged like a checkerboard. The motif is repeated in the window screens, *below right*.

The seating banquettes are upholstered foam rectangles set into stainless steel frames. These are upholstered in black fabric. All of the accessories in the room are also black.

The streamlined setting of the living room is hidden from view of the foyer by a wall divider, *top left*. Its massive surface and black color contrast in scale with the low furniture.

The dining area, *lower left*, continues the two-tone color scheme. The table top is set on two curved plexiglass

bases. For contrast, the Eames chairs are covered in white vinyl and two large antique paintings are predominantly dark in tone.

PHOTOS: CARLA DE BENEDETTI

207

IN THIS APARTMENT in Milan, one vibrant color is used against the white-painted glossy walls and black ceiling. The banquette is composed of cube forms upholstered in a bright, red-and-white striped fabric. Architect Claudio Dini used the same furniture forms and white Formica surfacing on cantilevered shelves throughout the space. The carpet, a high-pile fabric, underscores both the living and dining areas.

The alcove off the dining area, *bottom right,* continues the basic colors and furnishings to give the space visual unity. Note the lighting fixtures, down lights positioned with symmetrical precision in the spaces.

The bed area, *top left,* reverses the color scheme and the usual loft-bed arrangement. Here, the ceilings are painted glossy red and the bed cover utilizes a red-and-white striped fabric. The bed is placed on the floor level and a study loft is suspended above it.

Tableware, *bottom left,* echoes the basic two-color palette. Paneled doors behind the banquette and dividing the foyer area from the living room hide storage spaces.

PHOTOS: CARLA DE BENEDETTI

THE AUSTERE LOOK of this converted farmhouse in Ireland resembles that of an ancient stone monastery. Yet the house is far from forbidding. The dining room, *far left*, extends a sense of shelter with the stucco walls and fine selection of peasant furniture. Through the open doorway, the room overlooks a garden courtyard, which is paved with huge stones.

The house's owner is Irish artist Patrick Scott, who has used his artist's sensitivity to fill the house with tiny but superb arrangements. The series of vignettes, *right*, illustrates some of them: the kitchen utensils stored in earthenware pots, shelves in a wall niche displaying kitchen necessities, and the table top surrounded by two blue-and-white plaid-seat chairs.

The plate rack, *lower left*, an antique Irish example, has the severe lines typical of American Shaker furniture.

PHOTOS: NORMAN McGRATH

THE ATTIC of an older building in Rome yielded the space for this superb apartment. Architect Gae Aulenti redesigned the space to capitalize on its location and to bring in the view. A new skylight brings light down into the interiors while windows, mere sheets of glass, create the effect of a mural of Roman rooftops rimming the living room. Purposely, the furnishings in the room are subdued. A pair of white sofas face each other; one is set against an exposed brick wall, *left.*

The dining area, *top right,* has one wall of exposed brick and a new fireplace, surfaced in stucco. The effect of the putty-colored stucco and brick is to enhance the room's natural accents, such as the bleached wood dining table, canvas sling dining chairs, and sisal floor coverings.

A glimpse of the spectacular view from this attic space is seen in the vignette.

PHOTOS: EMMETT BRIGHT

The dining room, *left,* is rimmed by a low, carpeted ledge that is both a display surface and the base for banquette cushions. The dining table appears to be part of the cantilevered steps, which lead up to the small monastic bedroom, *right.*

In another view of the dining room, *lower left,* the treatment of the steps is shown as they traverse a small window. Against the wall the ledge is raised over storage units.

The bedroom, *right,* was distinguished by the vaulted ceiling, which architect Aulenti emphasized by painting it grey, the color of stone. A built-in closet echoes the curved ceiling line, *top right.* The bed rests on a low platform with storage drawers beneath and a small bookshelf beside it.

PHOTOS: EMMETT BRIGHT

THE SCALE of the furnishings—
the huge painting, towering
cactus, and primitive sculpture
—are keys to this apartment's drama.
It is the Paris home of Mrs. Ray-
monde Zenacker, designed by Fran-
çois Catroux. The geometric rug
surfacing the entire apartment underscores the cubic forms of the furniture. Blue-and-white colors, repeated
in the rug, banquettes, ottomans, and
easy chairs, are offset by the polished
steel accents of the fireplace surround, cube tables, and a ledge that
runs under the window. The fireplace
paneling is seen in the view of the
living room, *bottom right.*

The dining room, *top right,* combines
Eames chairs in blue leather with a
steel-top table on a pedestal base.
A banquette sits on the steel ledge
beside the fireplace in the adjoining
living room. On the back wall, glass
shelves on metal standards display
African art.

The foyer, *vignette,* provides visitors
with this garden view.

PHOTOS: PRIMOIS-PINTO

The white-lacquered chest and countertop links the bathroom with the bedroom to form a dressing area in the Zenacker apartment, *right*. On the far wall, over the bathtub, is hung a serigraph by artist Victor Vasarely. It adds vibrant color to the sapphire blue-and-white scheme.

A mirrored wall, *lower left*, reflects the bed and the low bedside table. The other walls are covered in a matte finish blue fabric.

The foyer, *top left*, is dramatically dark except for the two umbrella stands in white plastic, seen in the foreground.

PHOTOS: PRIMOIS-PINTO

A DELICATE BALANCE of objects and space creates a harmony in this small cottage in the south of France. Van Day Truex, for years an unofficial arbiter of American taste, owns and decorated the house. As the Dean of the Parsons School of Design for nearly thirty years and also as the design director of Tiffany & Co., both in New York, Mr. Truex has long been an influence in American design.

For his own residence, he has chosen the simplest of elements, rattan chairs and sofas, French provincial tables. In the living room, *top left and right*, the dark woods of the antique tables and twin lamps on either side of the rattan sofa are masterful accents to the neutral color scheme. The simple mirror is perfect for its location because of its fine proportions.

The dining room, *lower right*, continues the living room's simple furnishings yet it hardly lacks charm. Around the mirror over the serving shelf are displayed small faience plates, which are also delightfully arranged on the fireplace mantel.

The bedroom, *lower left*, is bare as a monk's cell. A provincial table is used with rattan chair across the room from the small bed.

PHOTOS: MICHAEL BOYS

THE INTERIOR of the Milanese apartment, *top right*, is capricious in quality. There is nothing stark or formal about its decorative treatment. Upholstered foam slabs in amorphous shapes are the chaise longue and chairs in the all-white room. The table is painted with the design of a cigarette logo. Another pop art touch is the painting over the fireplace. The room was designed by architects Fabrizio Paris and Patrizia Pietrogrande.

A mural of stylized trees creates another living room with a playful spirit, *lower right*. The chairs and ottomans of the modular sofa are strewn with colorful pillows and lighted by chrome, goose-neck lamps. The designer of the room was architect Claudio Dini.

Designer Nanda Vigo used a checkerboard motif in different sizes and colors to enliven this bedroom in Rome, *left*. The checks painted on the walls of the room merge into wide stripes; others are used in the bedspread design.

PHOTOS: CARLA DE BENEDETTI

THERE IS A MASCULINE STRENGTH and boldness about this London apartment, designed by Joseph Braswell. The mood results from the color palette of grey flannel fabric, polished steel accents, and the touches of red-leather upholstery. The fireplace wall, *right*, typifies Mr. Braswell's use of unconventional materials and styles. Although the mantel is an ornate marble antique, it is surrounded by a panel of polished steel. A round niche displays a Roman bust.

Two identical sofas are placed back-to-back, with a table in between, *top left*, to divide the large room into two seating areas. A polished steel etagère is flanked by shuttered windows. Two red-leather covered *bergères* are used around an antique French table, *lower left*.

PHOTOS: NORMAN MCGRATH

Designer Joseph Braswell proves himself a master at the controlled use of pattern. In the bedroom, *left*, he introduces a small-scale floral repeat as the fabric for the bed canopy and also to cover the small sofa. On the walls is another pattern, a subdued stripe, while on the floors the pattern grows bolder, a geometric repeat. Color binds the diverse patterns together; all the prints share a blue-and-white palette.

Charcoal brown walls and shutters offset the white marble countertop in the bathroom, *right*. The shaving mirror is suspended from the ceiling on brass rods. Other brass and gold accessories, such as the fixtures, basin, towel rack, and soap dishes, are sumptuous touches.

PHOTOS: NORMAN McGRATH

THE BATHROOM in this vacation cottage in the south of France is remarkable for its architecture and its size. Both are enhanced by the placement of the tub in the room's center between the deeply set windows.

The dining room, *far right and vignette*, has the rustic charm befitting a country house. The roof is made up of rough, split-wood beams. All of the furniture is simple in outline, a farmhouse table and ladderback chairs. The carved hobby horse, standing on a window ledge beside the fireplace, typifies the house's personal accessories.

Lighted open shelves create a storage niche for dishes in the pantry, which adjoins the kitchen area, *lower right*.

The diagonal of the slate floors inset with wood strips puts pattern underfoot in the living room, *far right*. A baroque mirror tops the French mantel. Two plump sofas stand in front of the fireplace.

PHOTOS: TIM STREET-PORTER

THE BOLD DESIGN of the striped carpeting that surfaces all of the floors is a unifying element in this London apartment. The carpet begins in the foyer, *center*, crosses the living and dining rooms, *far right*, and continues into the bedroom, *below*, and bathroom, *vignette*. Against the black-and-beige tones of the carpeting, beige and green accents are used exclusively. Most of the furniture used in the space is built-in. The seating banquettes in the living room are raised on a carpeted platform and covered in a chamois-colored fabric. The bed is accented by a black-painted wall and is reached by steps.

Shadows from the louvered shutters, *top far right*, repeat and echo the diagonal theme of the carpeting. The effect is illustrated in this view, where floor-to-ceiling bookcases line the walls and the windows are covered by a Roman shade.

PHOTOS: GRAHAM HENDERSON

230

THIS INTERIOR in Milan expresses the elegance of a black, white, and red color scheme. It was designed by architect Claudio Dini. The round shape of the lighting fixtures is repeated in the drum tables and columns of the interior architecture. The kitchen, *lower right*, is situated in the wide corridor adjoining the dining area. To disguise the utilitarian aspect of the kitchen, the cabinet doors are painted glossy black. They contrast with the light walls and furniture of the living room, *top right*. A built-in banquette, covered in persimmon colored velvet, hugs a curving wall. Over the banquette, bookshelves repeat the curve.

The study area, *top*, is loosely separated from the living room by the two round columns holding bookshelves.

Stainless steel edges the countertops and cabinets of the kitchen. Appliances are also surfaced in sleek stainless steel.

PHOTOS: CARLA DE BENEDETTI

THE TOTAL REDESIGN of an existing attic resulted in this handsome duplex apartment in Milan. The most arresting feature is the new loft, *top right,* which is both a study-bedroom and a sitting room. The shiny wall surfaces articulate the new interior architecture and are offset by the black-toned furnishings and carpeting.

A wide terrace garden surrounds the living area on the lower floor, *bottom right.* The floor-to-ceiling glass doors open it to both the living room and adjoining dining alcove. The structural column becomes a graphic motif in the space. At the base, it is surrounded by a table surface.

Although the dining room is sleekly modern, *top left,* it is enhanced by the use of antique Italian chairs around the glass table. Beside the built-in storage cabinet is another antique, a tall pedestal column.

Even the kitchen, *lower left,* mixes sleek architecture with antique accents, such as the two paintings and pair of painted urns on the countertop, shown in this setting.

PHOTOS: LO STUDIO

BRONZE-TINTED MIRRORS lend a luxurious air to this bathroom in London, *left*. The mirrors surface two of the room's four walls and also surround the bathtub and a utility column. The wheat-colored carpet, black chair with caned seat, and the basket used as a hamper are simple, natural accents to the elegant scheme.

The bedroom in the same flat, *right*, attracts the eye with the arresting modern painting by Helen Frankenthaler, *vignette*. The painting dominates one wall near the entrance. In the bedroom proper, the bed stands alone; while a large chair, shaped like a baseball mitt, is in the adjacent sitting area, *lower right*.

Beige draperies are used on several walls to soften the severity of the room's furnishings. The dressing area, *far right*, is situated in the corridor linking the bedroom and bathroom.

PHOTOS: TIM STREET-PORTER

THIS VACATION HOUSE enjoys a stunning view of the Mediterranean through the living room window. The tropical flavor is brought indoors by the use of tall palms and the pastel color palette. The seating banquette is covered in upholstery fabric of light green, while the dining room chairs are upholstered in melon-colored leather. The white walls, ottomans, and sand-colored carpeting all convey the mood of a sophisticated, yet relaxed, vacation retreat.

A secondary dining room and game room, *top right*, is set in the midst of an indoor garden. Trellis screens and a canvas cover over the skylight can shut out the worst of the sun's rays during the day.

The dining area is situated in the ell of the living room. The glass-top table has a travertine base and is surrounded by the bamboo chairs. A mirrored wall niche stores glasses for the bar.

PHOTOS: EMMETT BRIGHT

239

THE WHITE-PAINTED round posts supporting the roof are a recurring decorative and structural motif in this remarkable house. It was designed by Italian architect Gae Aulenti and it has the mood of a house in the tropics. Windows are covered with trellissed screens, *top right,* which add to this ambiance.

The living room, *left,* is furnished with a single design of a chair and ottoman, a single lamp design, and the modern glass-top table. The repetition of these three elements throughout the space accounts for the room's feeling of order and spaciousness.

The sleekness of the dining area, *lower right,* results from the unusual table and seating design. The table is a wide slab top on a base with flush sides, and the seating for it is a bench instead of individual chairs. The partial divider screens the kitchen from view.

The bathroom, *vignette,* merges with the bedroom space. The separation of these two areas is loosely defined by the back of the washbasin counter and the hanging mirror.

PHOTOS: EMMETT BRIGHT

A BRASS FOUR-POSTER bed and shirred walls, *right*, create a setting with a Directoire flavor. Modern paintings and art and the stark outlines of the contemporary bedside tables leaven the traditional mood. The horn-covered cube table at the foot of the bed rests on a geometric-patterned rug.

Another bedroom in Rome, *top left*, enjoys a view of St. Peter's Cathedral in the distance. The interior scheme of the room is purposely played down to complement the view. The oyster white wall color is repeated in the fabric of the bed canopy and the draperies. A contemporary patchwork quilt adds a blue accent to the neutral color scheme.

A pair of Indian wood chairs, painted white, and the bamboo furniture are exotic touches in the white bedroom, *lower left*. The bed has an all-upholstered frame. Two bookcases are set into deep recesses on either side of the doorways. The ceiling fan is both practical and decorative.

PHOTOS: EMMETT BRIGHT

THE ANCIENT OVERHEAD BEAMS, the fireplace, and the tiled floors attest to the medieval age of this building. It is the interior of the Castello di Monte Savello in Italy. The furnishings are also medieval in flavor, the long refectory dining table has a church pew bench as dining seats and two small side chairs.

Although sparsely furnished, the bedroom is nontheless calm and enchanting. That ambiance extends from the beautiful, wide arched windows, the ceiling beams, the tiled floor, and the room's grand size. The Italian antique bed frame has baroque spiral turned posts.

PHOTOS: LO STUDIO

AMERICAN MODERN

A MERICAN INTERIORS have been moving toward ever greater sophistication, deriving from even greater simplification. Furniture and clutter is disappearing. Tables full of objects, in fact, even tables themselves, have disappeared altogether in many living environments. Furniture is merging with the architecture. Seating is becoming soft, comfortable forms of no particular style, simply loose pillows, low banquettes, and ottomans, superbly tailored and supremely inviting.

Comfort as well as easy maintenance is all-important in contemporary interior design. The neutral and all-white interior is very popular, and thanks to miracle finishes that are resistant to stains and soils, it can be designed to answer both needs. Industrial materials are taking on a new role in residential design—and look elegantly suited to it. Conversely, the natural accent—cane, bamboo, sisal, hemp, raw wood—is still highly desirable. And so are plants, which provide both the warmth of living, growing things and the punch of sculpture in today's room schemes.

Americans desire low maintenance but they want it to be stylish. So, designers have come up with interiors that derive their elegance from understatement. It's a case of subtraction in today's spaces rather than addition: subtracting the clutter and distraction of furniture, objects, and pattern. There's less rather than more of everything. Space and its quality of light are the most significant elements in today's serene spaces.

California interiors have a special signature. They are a blend of the beams and tiled floors of Spanish architecture and accents from nature. Designer Jay Steffy of Los Angeles is a master at bringing together modern design with a southwest flavor. The mood is expressed in this sophisticated, yet casual, living room.

PHOTO: JAY STEFFY

THE LIVING ROOM combines the easy, unstudied shapes of contemporary upholstery with a monochromatic color palette. Jay Steffy dramatized the massiveness of the ceiling beams by keeping everything else in the room low in height and light in scale. The furniture is nothing more than amorphous forms, round chairs and banquettes that look like big pillows. Bamboo blinds are hung below the rounded arches of the windows.

The stucco walls and arched doorways of the house's architecture, *right*, provided suitable contrast for Steffy's furniture selection: the tree trunk used as the console table in the foyer, topped by the modern painting.

Two more curved doorways, *vignettes*, frame the pool room and the bar, where the outline of a curved banquette echoes the arches. The bar is encircled by director chairs used as bar stools.

PHOTOS: JAY STEFFY

THIS LIVING ROOM in Southampton, Long Island, expresses the power of space and light on an interior scheme. Designer John Saladino capitalized on the room's high ceiling and its large window by keeping the rest of the furniture in the room extremely low and light in tone. There is an absence of anything jarring to disturb the room's spatial quality or softness of light.

Both walls and furniture covers are white, *left*. The floors and the cube coffee table are covered in sisal carpeting. Saladino designed the couch as a daybed with upholstered sides accented by rolled bolsters. Another couch, also covered in white fabric, stands across the room. Two large plants are positioned like sculpture on either side of the window.

In contrast to the rest of the room's light palette, the fireplace hearth is painted dark, *right*. Upholstered panels and doors conceal storage spaces around the fireplace.

The vignette, *lower right,* emphasizes the scheme's effective use of natural materials for accent: beside the couch is a lighted cube table, cane-and-steel occasional chair, and hanging plant.

PHOTOS: NORMAN MCGRATH

THE EFFECTIVENESS of using a minimum of two colors to create a color scheme is shown in this Long Island living room, designed by Joseph D'Urso. Nothing could be simpler than its monochrome coloration: white walls, slate gray carpeting, gray leather sofas, set in black enameled wood frames. But the room does not lack for color. The large canvas in red, yellow, and green on the wall introduces the splash of strong primary color. Natural accents also soften the hard edges of the basic black-and-white scheme. Placed on either side of the back-to-back sofas, which divide the large room into conversation areas, are steel-and-cane chairs, baskets, Oriental rugs, and large plants.

PHOTOS: PETER AARON

A N UNDULATING BANQUETTE, covered in white vinyl fabric, becomes a piece of environmental furniture in this country house in Ireland. It was designed by architect Sam Stephenson for his family. The architect used the modern furniture forms to update the old architecture. The banquette provides both the room's seating and also its table surfaces. The back is rigid enough to support objects. A cantilevered shelf spans an existing arched wall niche. It becomes the surface for bar accessories and to display art works.

In another older building, *top left,* built around the turn-of-the-century in New York, designer Tom Britt used a muted color scheme and modern furnishings to complement the architecture. Against the soft tones of gray walls and the dark floors, the white sofa and elegant steel cocktail tables appear to float in space.

The dining area of the same apartment, *lower left,* is furnished with a curved built-in banquette. The glass top of the dining table echoes that curve. Flattering the room's existing paneling are the chamois colored walls and upholstery of the banquette. Across the room from the fireplace is a sofa, which is backed by a tortoise-shell covered sofa table.

PHOTOS: LEFT, RICHARD CHAMPION; RIGHT, NORMAN MCGRATH

Once again, greenhouses are becoming an important part of today's architecture. Similar in purpose to the conservatory of Victorian times, they are partly to enjoy and cultivate plants, partly to purify the air (plants absorb carbon dioxide), and partly for people to luxuriate in the lushness of a year-round garden.

Those three purposes are provided by this greenhouse, which opens off of the French doors of the living room. In the lush spaces amidst the plantings is a hammock and table for relaxing.

Tall windows of the living room, *bottom right,* contribute to the room's remarkable quality of light. On the table surfaces the owner's have arranged their collection of small art objects, such as the pre-Columbian figures

The dining room, *top right,* opens out to the landscaped grounds through French doors. In contrast to the airiness provided by the windows, the fireplace hearth is made to seem deep, enclosed, sheltered by the extension of the new wall around it.

PHOTOS: PETER AARON

257

DESIGNER WARD BENNETT'S
beach house in Amagansett,
Long Island, is a chameleon
that changes according to the seasons.
In summer it is an open air pavilion.
Exterior sections of the house walls
actually swing away like giant doors
merging the indoor spaces with the
outside. A huge skylight also floods
the interiors with light. It can be
shaded from the sun's direct rays by
sliding accordion-pleated blinds.

In winter the orientation of the house
turns from the outdoors to the inside
spaces. The walls remain closed
and the house revolves around the
fireplace, which is raised on a platform and set against a background of
black metal walls. The room's wood
paneling contributes a sense of
shelter and enclosure.

PHOTOS: ERNST BEADLE

INTERIOR DESIGN has been moving in the direction of greater flexibility in furniture arrangement—furniture that moves around to form different seating arrangements to suit different needs. Robert Patino designed a modular seating system for his New York apartment, *left*. The seating system is composed of chaise longues, ottomans, and corner chairs, which he rearranges at will. The leather-covered units and the low, black marble cocktail tables furnish the entire room. The background, too, is low key: the fireplace wall is mirrored, *top right*, the windows are covered with vertical blinds, and the floors are surfaced in sisal carpeting.

Limited edition photographic prints by Richard Avedon provide the room's only art. A torso of Andy Warhol is reflected in the fireplace mirror and another Avedon portrait is hung in the arched doorway of the hall, *vignette, far left*.

In the kitchen, *vignette*, a dining counter is set with Breuer cane chairs beneath a plant-filled window. Mirrored doors update the cabinets.

The canopy bed, which is draped in monk's cloth, creates a fantasy world in the bedroom, *lower right*. It is reflected endlessly in the mirrored folding screen behind a slipper chair.

PHOTOS: FRANK KELLEOGY

INDUSTRIAL MATERIALS and products are finding their way into home decoration. This apartment, the home of a young advertising executive, Faith Popcorn, is studded with products from industry—commercial kitchen shelves, restaurant table bases, a file cabinet used as an end table—yet these add to rather than detract from the room's sophistication. Because the owner needed both living and work-at-home space, designers Bray-Schaible hid the Murphy bed in a cabinet to devote most of the L-shaped studio to sitting and dining.

A carpeted platform extends across one wall, *right,* and holds the seating banquette; it continues past the banquette as a low display ledge. A standard drafting-plan file cabinet, in a white enamel finish, makes an elegant side table as well as providing needed storage space.

Two leather chairs, *top left,* augment the room's seating. The round drum from Thailand, placed in front of the banquette, serves as an additional table surface near the chairs. It stands on top of the pony skin rug. The Ming tree in the corner adds the garnish of live greenery to the subtle color scheme.

Across the room, *bottom left,* industrial wire shelves, which are standard equipment in commercial kitchens, create a storage wall behind the dining table. The tabletop is a slab of limestone mounted on two restaurant metal bases. The four rattan chairs are used as dining seats. The large table is ideal as a work space as well as for dining.

PHOTOS: RICHARD CHAMPION

262

ANTIQUES ARE USED to accent this contemporary scheme, in an apartment for a young couple involved in the theater. It was designed by Paul van Eyre. A built-in banquette rims the window wall, a game table is positioned in the room's center surrounded by antique Biedermeier armchairs. The fireplace wall has another juxtaposition of antique and modern: the Biedermeier secretary paired with a Breuer tubular-steel desk chair, *top left*.

The foyer is a study in recurrent curves—from the round painting by Poleskie and the lines of the Empire loveseat, *top right*. The bar area, *lower right*, has wire drain racks (the kind generally used above the sink) hung as shelves for glasses. Utilitarian as they are, the shelves are elegant in this setting.

The large dining room, *lower left*, is set up at one end as a library/study. There is a raised carpeted platform and pillows for lounging. The shelves store hi-fi equipment, records, and books.

PHOTOS: PAUL VANEYRE

I T IS AN ALL-PURPOSE ROOM, part culinary work center furnished with appliances of restaurant quality and part sewing center and home office. That was the concept behind this kitchen, planned and owned by restaurateur Georg Lang and his wife Karen. Both are avid cooks, George specializes in the Hungarian dishes of his childhood and Karen in all types of baked delectables.

The restaurant range and its copper hood is the room's hub of cooking activity. Everything radiates around it. Butcher block counters extend on three of the room's walls around the range, with copious storage cabinets both above and below. The cupboards have arched glass doors to keep the contents on the shelves in view and to save searching.

The service pass-through to the dining room adjoins the kitchen work center. Against the far wall, with the blue-tiled backsplash, is a special area for baking. The countertop there is marble, above drawers compartmentalized into bins for sugar, flour, and baking necessities. The large double-door restaurant refrigerator, sheathed in stainless steel, is placed midway between the range and the baking center to be convenient to both.

The range front, *top vignette*, is sheathed in copper like the hood. The counters of the office and sewing center are also topped in butcher block. The doorway beyond the range looks through to the dining area, where the mahogany table is surrounded by red-seated chairs.

PHOTOS: NORMAN MCGRATH

HIGH ABOVE MANHATTAN is this remarkable environment, a serene fortress removed from the bustle on the city streets below. It is the home of a young couple, the Mark Perlbinders, and was designed by John Saladino, who changed the floor plan and materials so drastically that the interiors no longer resemble the typical high-rise plan. By removing walls, the designer created vistas through all of the rooms. From the kitchen, *left*, the space flows past the dining room and into the study unobstructed. The eat-in area of the kitchen (foreground) pairs a rustic antique farmhouse table with modern dining chairs.

The dining room, *top right*, uses color subtly. Through the opening into the foyer, there is a glimpse of a bright orange wall. The sliding glass doors that close off the study are painted yellow. The dining table is a stone slab set on a pedestal base. The chairs have tubular steel frames with cane basket seats. On the wall is a silk prayer rug.

By raising the living room seating area on a platform, Saladino brought the city into the view of those seated on the suede-covered sofas. There is another bench for seating directly beneath the window. Two rattan chairs with yellow cushions introduce the vibrant accent color to the monochromatic color scheme.

PHOTOS: NORMAN McGRATH

Upon entering the Perlbinder apartment, the impact of the new interior architecture is apparent. New floor surfaces are planks laid on the diagonal and accented by the Oriental rug. The ceiling of stainless steel panels creates the effect of a mirror overhead, doubling the height of the space by reflection. The carpeted steps lead up to the living room platform.

The series of vignettes, *right,* depict the meticulous detailing of the apartment. The stainless steel ceiling and its dramatic reflections continues into the bar area (largest picture). Also seen is the new kitchen with walls lined with natural wood cabinetry; a bench installed beneath the window in the bathroom; the bed in the master bedroom against a diagonally placed wall; and the view of the East River that the apartment enjoys from the living room window.

PHOTOS: NORMAN MCGRATH

THE APARTMENT of fashion designer Chester Weinberg is a place of great style resulting from very few objects, chosen with extraordinary selectivity. The designer, Joseph D'Urso achieved this sophistication by using products from industry with modern furniture classics.

The living room has no sofa. Instead, an upholstered pad and pillows for lounging are laid atop a carpeted platform. Two laminated wood lounge chairs, designed by architect Alvar Aalto, are used with a low, black, Formica-top table mounted on a metal restaurant base. The lighting in the room is supplied by the white, metal factory lamps, hung from the ceiling tracks. In contrast to the living room's lightness, the foyer walls are painted black. The door between the two rooms was removed, *lower left,* to play up that contrast between the small, dark foyer space and the white-walled living room.

Another view of the living room, *top right,* looks from the carpeted platform into the bedroom, which continues the same color scheme. Notice how the platform becomes a table surface for holding drinks, an ash-tray, or in this setting, a black tray holding a still-life arrangement of a plant and sculpture. The arrangement is highlighted by the beam of the factory lamp.

Another restaurant-base table, *lower right,* is spread with a Kilim rug and encircled by two black draftsmen's chairs.

The windows are covered with vertical blinds.

PHOTOS: RICHARD CHAMPION

THE CITY APARTMENT of jewelry designer Elsa Peretti is marked by restrained elegance. It is a study in minimal elegance, "no-nonsense chic." Bob Patino designed the one-bedroom space in answer to her request for a place of great elegance that was also easy to maintain. The floors are bleached and polyurethaned and all of the furniture slip-covers come off for washing.

Although the apartment is small, Patino made it seem much larger by the use of mirrors. In the living room, *top left,* mirrored panels extend behind the banquette across the entire wall and turn the corner. The illusion is that the space continues on and on. The dining room is seen through the doorway. It is separated from the kitchen door by a folding screen, which can be seen in a close-up view, *bottom right.* On the dining table, is a collection of pots holding work brushes and pencils. Many of the porcelain pots and vases, *vignette, far right,* were picked up on a recent trip to China.

The bedroom, *lower left,* echoes the living room in color scheme, furnishings, and use of mirrors. During parties, the guests use it as a secondary living room. The large sofa, piled with pillows, is actually a double-size bed. Vertical blinds are hung over the windows on top of the built-in storage cabinet, which is faced in white Formica.

Mirrored panels flank either side of the fireplace, *top right,* and the foyer is furnished with a tree-trunk table, backed by a mirror. Elsa's silver sculpture is arranged with votive candles on a counter top.

PHOTOS: FRANK KELLEOGY

274

THE PLAYFUL INTERIORS of this house complement its seaside setting on the New Jersey coast. The living room is both chic and easy to care for. The modular seating group that forms the long banquette, *left*, is covered in wipe-off vinyl fabric. The three lounge chairs and the occasional tables are all made of washable, high-impact-proof plastic. Colorful pillows enliven the all-white scheme. The modern painting hung high up on the wall that looks like a wrinkled beach towel, adds the splash of stripes.

Another view, *top right*, emphasizes the sculptural quality of the architecture: the storage wall and the staircase behind it. The ocean vista is seen through the sliding glass doors. Both the house and its interiors were designed by architect Gus Wormuth.

The dining room, living room, and kitchen share essentially one large space. The kitchen area is screened from the view of the dining area by a partial divider. The back of the living room banquette also creates a visual division between the two areas. The dining room table is an oval plastic top on a pedestal base, surrounded by molded plastic pedestal chairs. Both table and chairs were designed by Eero Saarinen.

PHOTOS: GIL AMIAGA

WITHIN THE CONFINES of a typical high-rise building, designer Joseph D'Urso has created an apartment of great spatial beauty. It is the home of designer Calvin Klein in New York. D'Urso applied one of his basic design tenets in planning the space. He believes in "subtracting," or removing all of the false walls, dropped ceilings, superfluous doors until he arrives at the structural bones of the building itself. Within the outline of the new-found perimeter, D'Urso redesigns the space, creating new walls and openings where necessary and creating seating areas, such as the banquettes that wrap around corners.

PHOTOS: PETER AARON

The interiors of the Calvin Klein apartment are a study in monotones and minimal furnishings. There are only two colors used in the space, the glossy white of the walls and the slate grey of the carpeting and black leather banquettes. Only a single table and chair design is used as well: the black leather-and-chrome lounge chair and the chrome-and-glass table. The windows are covered with vertical blinds. The long banquette terminates around the corner of the living room, *top left,* next to the small bar. That bar is painted shiny black, in contrast to the living room's whiteness, and to accent the glitter of the glassware displayed on open shelves.

Instead of doors, D'Urso designed pivoting wall panels to close off the bedroom from the hallway of the living area. There are two such swinging walls in the apartment. Another, *bottom right,* closes off the dining alcove from the bedroom-study.

D'Urso is one of the leading proponents of using industrial materials at home. Notice the swinging door (extreme left of photo, bottom right), which leads into the kitchen. This is a standard restaurant door of stainless steel, light in weight, and pierced by a rounded window. How elegant it appears in the company of such sophisticated design.

PHOTOS: PETER AARON

TRANQUIL, easy to maintain, stripped down to essentials—this apartment in Manhattan overlooking Central Park is very much today. It was designed by Poppy Wolff and Bray-Schaible for a publicist, Mrs. Maraleita Dutton Herbert. The modular seating units combine to make two sofas, placed back-to-back and also are used alone as single chairs. Although they look fragile, the white covers on the seating units are Scotchguarded and removable for cleaning.

PHOTO: NORMAN McGRATH

Because the living room was exceedingly long, the designers divided it into two areas by placing modular seating sofas back-to-back in its center. One area is ideal for group relaxing, while the other ('background) seats two or three comfortably in rattan chairs around a game table. The linen rug, white bamboo blinds at the windows, and the white Formica shelf that rims the room, all serve to bind the two areas together visually.

An antique Kilim rug leads from the entry door into the living room, *top left*. The door opening between the dining room and hallway is spanned by a new Formica shelf that acts as the console table for the foyer. Two x-base stools, covered in suede, stand beneath it.

The round Formica-top table in the dining room, *bottom right*, is encircled by eight suede-covered chairs.

An Amish appliqué quilt is framed and hung on the wall like a painting. Storage cabinets support the service shelf in the door opening.

PHOTOS: NORMAN McGRATH

THE 18-FOOT-HIGH CEILINGS of this living room in Manhattan gave its owners, Mr. and Mrs. Ernest Rubenstein, the space to hang their large modern canvases. The paintings and the Oriental rug infuse the room with color, although most of the furniture—the Eames lounge chair and two sofas—are neutral beige leather. Over the banquette is a painting by Van Deren and over the hearth, one by Okada. What appears to be a folding screen in the corner is an art work by Jim Dine.

Part of this interior's delight derives from the way designer Lila Schneider contrasted the spare functional lines of modern art with the naive country crafted furniture. In the foyer, *top right,* a modern painting of polyester by Tony Palladino is hung above a Victorian settee. The glass doors open onto the dining room.

Natural wood Breuer dining chairs are used with an old farmhouse table, *bottom right,* their raw woods complementing each other. The painting by Santé Graziani adds the smash of bold graphics to the scheme.

PHOTOS: JOHN VELTRI

The dining room is set up both for dining and for relaxing. Behind the table is a leather couch, easy chair and an Oriental rug. The white ceiling and white light tracks give the room an airy quality.

The kitchen, *below left,* is a meld of natural accents and bold graphics. The open shelves and dining table are slabs of butcher block. The floor is covered in tiny hexagonal tiles. Thin venetian blinds at the windows, the wall clock and perpetual calendar are contemporary accents.

The living room's distinction derives from the mix of rustic forms with modern furniture and art. For instance, an early American red-painted cupboard stands next to the foyer door between the two large modern art works. Another antique, a Victorian settee, is seen through the archway in the foyer. Either side of the fireplace has built-in banquettes with cushions covered in fragments of Kilim rugs.

PHOTOS: JOHN VELTRI

T̲HE INTERIOR of this loft proves
once again that sophistication
can derive from the most hum-
ble of objects. Nothing in this space
is costly and, in fact, many of the
elements used here are quite ordinary.
Yet the ambiance and visual effect
of the space is one of distinction.

The loft was designed and built by
its owner, Jack Ceglic, an artist who
both lives and works here. The main
living area shares its space with
the artist's studio (not shown). The
existing columns are used to loosely
define the space into the seating area
and the bedroom. The seating is provided by large floor pillows, which
are backed by low tables.

The dining table, *below,* was a work
table left over from the days when
the loft was a toy factory. Ceglic
stripped it down to its raw wood,
which yielded the rich patina. The
dining chairs are Mexican rawhide-
and-wood imports. Plants give the
huge loft the fresh feeling of a greenhouse.
PHOTOS: JAMES MATHEWS

INTEREST IN the 1920s and 1930s has revived a taste for the angular forms and pastel color schemes of the Art Deco period. This bedroom and bathroom, designed by Tom Booth, expresses a new interpretation of that style. An existing fireplace was mirrored with circular panels, which are Art Deco in outline. The mirrors reflect the bed across the room, which is raised on a platform and carpeted the same tone as the floor.

The bed, seen in the vignette, *far left*, is flanked by the black-lacquered Deco-style table.

The 1930s color scheme of mauves and orange tints carries through into the bathroom, *right*. Here, the walls are sheathed in wood paneling, laid on the diagonal, to update the old-fashioned bathroom. Other modernizing touches are the new metal shower curtain bar and the light strip over the basin area.

PHOTOS: ROBERT PERRON

THE GARDEN LEVEL of a city brownstone was remodeled into this informal, living/dining room/kitchen, a sleeker version of the old-fashioned family room. The redesign was done by architects Armstrong-Childs for Mr. and Mrs. Marshall Allen. All the walls that had separated the space into small rooms were removed to create one large room. Sliding glass doors were installed to open onto the back garden.

The kitchen area, *top right,* juxtaposes the warmth of the wood cabinets with the shiny efficient look of the stainless steel appliances. The area beneath the cabinet, *bottom right,* displays a collection of Mrs. Allen's small artifacts, framed butterflies, antique pottery, and kitchen essentials such as spice bottles.

The wood kitchen cabinets are so well detailed that they suit the living room area as well as the kitchen. Here, *top left,* they hold stereo equipment and records. The top shelves display baskets and art.

The semi-circular end of the kitchen counter, *bottom left,* creates a transition from the living area into the dining area, and also, into the living area. The curve of the counter is echoed overhead in the dropped ceiling that hides the room's lighting. Built-in banquettes wrap around the counter and the wall to face the fireplace.

PHOTOS: ROBERT PERRON

MODERN ART lines the walls of the double-height space in a California beach house, *left*. Huge plants add the punch of sculptural forms. The room hardly looks decorated, rather it looks as though the objects were selected by personal conviction and choice.

Two bedrooms by Jay Steffy, *right*, are arranged with a similar air of understated casualness. The one, *top right*, has natural accents of straw blinds and white duck upholstery on the banquettes. An overturned basket serves as the table.

The other bedroom, *below*, is furnished with only a brass bed and small rattan table. Its excitement derives from the painted ceiling. It is the outline of a large circle, rimmed by bands of color.

PHOTOS: JAY STEFFY

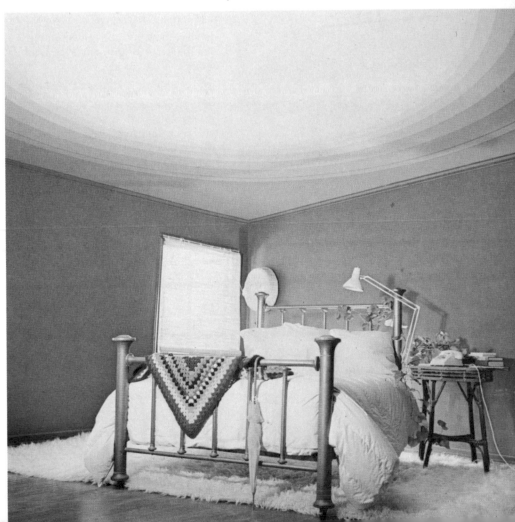

THIS BROOKLYN HEIGHTS apartment commands a superb view of New York bay. To bring that view within the gaze of those seated in the room, designer John Saladino raised the seating area on a curved platform. He also installed a wall of bronze-tinted mirror across one wall to reflect the view, *right*. The mirror wall also makes the long, narrow space appear to be much wider than it is.

A built-in banquette was installed beneath the windows as a place to dine, *top left*. Sliding stainless steel doors close off the kitchen from view, while their shiny surfaces reflect the harbor view to those seated on the banquette. A library-study area adjoins the dining alcove.

The round drum in the center of the living room serves two functions: it creates a small foyer area off the entrance door and is also fitted out as the bar, *middle*. Two carpeted cylinders are the bar stools.

PHOTOS: NORMAN McGRATH

THE SCULPTURAL INTERIORS of
this renovated building are as
much an art form as the art
collection of Mr. and Mrs. Bil
Ehrlich, for which the space was
redesigned. Mr. Ehrlich, an architect, first gutted and then reinstalled
the new interior levels. Although the
space appears complicated because
of the many interior wall openings, it
is quite simple. The building is now
essentially one large room, pierced
by two projecting balconies, one for
the kitchen and the one above it, for
the master bedroom. A 45-foot-long
skylight overlooks the levels from
above.

In the living room, *right,* four identical sofas float on the white poured
epoxy floors; they are surrounded
by art of the New York school, the
colorful swirls of the Frank Stella
painting on the side wall, next to
the 30-foot-high Donald Judd sculpture that scales the wall. (It is also
reflected in the coffee table.) The steel
construction on the floor, behind one
of the sofas is a sculpture by Tim
Scott. The first balcony that over-
hangs the living room space, holds
the kitchen.

The view from the stairwell, *bottom
left,* gives this vista of the living
room. The painting behind the sofa
is by Morris Louis. The skylight is
visible in this picture.

The staircase links the three-story-
high space, *right,* rising one level to
the kitchen and another level to the
master bedroom. The wall openings
or "interior windows" from those
levels overlook the living room.

PHOTOS: NORMAN McGRATH

300

The sitting room, *top left*, is actually
a gallery for art. Two swinging
chairs, made of see-through plastic,
hang from the ceiling, surrounded
by art, including the Andy Warhol
picture of Elvis Presley and a Ron
Davis painting.

A bright canvas in pastel yellows by
W. Darby Bannard, injects color
into the monochromatic scheme of
the dining room, *bottom left*. Architect Ehrlich designed the table, which
is a semi-circular chrome base with
a glass top. It is surrounded by four
Plya chairs imported from Italy.

The master bedroom, *bottom right*,
has a built-in platform which is inset
with the bed mattress so that they
appear at one level. The bathroom
shares the bedroom space. The
counter with twin washbasins is seen
in the foreground. The shower cabinet is actually a greenhouse which receives light from the skylight overhead, *top right*.

PHOTOS: NORMAN McGRATH

GLOSSARY
OF DECORATIVE
TERMS

Apron   That part of the chair or table connecting the legs; also called a "skirt."*

Armoire (French, pronounced "ar-mwahr")   A tall wardrobe with hinged front doors. It probably evolved from a cabinet used to store armor and arms. It is often painted or carved with elaborate front-door panels and has a bonnet* or pediment*top.

Aubusson   Fine antique carpets or tapestries in a flat weave, usually in pastel shades with stylized floral designs. They were made in a French village bearing the same name, beginning in the seventeenth century up until the present time.

Bachelor's chest   A low three- or four-drawer chest designed to house small items of male apparel. It evolved from a small-scale chest of the eighteenth century.

Ball or *bun foot*   A round turning at the bottom of a leg or chest. Frequently, the ball or bun foot is found on William and Mary furniture. The bun foot is a bit more flattened out than the ball foot.

Baluster   A spindle used to support a railing or intended for furniture legs as an ornament. It is more commonly known as a banister. A balustrade consists of a series of spindles or banisters.

Banding   A narrow strip of veneer inlay used to frame drawer fronts or tabletops. The wood grain of the banding usually runs counter to the surface veneer to provide for maximum contrast and decorative effect.

Banister back   High-backed chair produced in America during the late seventeenth century with the uprights of the back made from turned spindles.

Banquette (French, pronounced "bahn-ket")   An upholstered, built-in bench or seat usually containing no exposed wood frame.

Baroque (French, from the Spanish word *barrueco,* which means a large, irregularly shaped pearl)   A style of furniture and architecture originating in Italy in the sixteenth century which spread throughout Europe. It is characterized by exaggerated scale, fantastic curves, and bold detail. It was succeeded by the rococo* style.

---

* N.B. Asterisked entries are defined elsewhere in the Glossary.

Batik A print fabric produced by wax resist and successive dyeing or painting, based upon an old Javanese technique.

Beading A tiny semi-circular molding used to outline the edges of a drawer, usually found on eighteenth-century English and American furniture.

Bauhaus A school founded in Germany in 1919, which emphasized total design, i.e., an intermingling of all the design disciplines, including art, architecture, graphics, furniture, and industrial design. Founded by Walter Gropius, the school believed in designing for the newer forms of technology and mass production. The Bauhaus is often referred to as the seat of modern design.

Bergère (French, pronounced "bear-zhair") An armchair in the Louis XV and XVI styles with closed upholstered sides and back. See also *marquise*.

Bibliothèque (French, pronounced "biblioteck") A large architectural bookcase.

Biedermeier Provincial German version of the French Empire style. The name was derived from a popular comic-strip character of the time, Papa Biedermeier, who symbolized *gemütlichkeit* or homey comfort. Biedermeier was in fashion during the first half of the nineteenth century.

Bird's eye A decorative veneer composed of a mottled wood grain, usually maple, suggesting a bird's eye.

Blanket chest A deep, rustic wooden trunk mounted on a base that was used to store textiles and blankets during the American Colonial period.

Block front A design feature typical of chests produced by Newport, Rhode Island, furniture makers of the eighteenth century. The chest front is divided into three equal panels; the two end panels jut out while the center panel is recessed. The three panels are often topped by a carved shell, similarly convex and concave in design to echo the panels.

Boiserie (French, pronounced "bwa-ze-ree") Literally, woodwork. Specifically, the eighteenth-century French style of carved-wood paneling installed on all four walls of a room.

Bolection A robust projecting molding used to frame a fireplace or panel. Generally speaking, a fireplace with a bolection molding will not have a mantel.

Bombé (French, pronounced "bombay") The bulging front and/or sides on a chest, often seen on Louis XV, late eighteenth-century Italian, and Venetian furniture; also called "bowfront."

Bonnetière (French, pronounced "bon-et-eeair") A tall wardrobe that is normally half as wide as an armoire. It was used in the eighteenth century to store women's elaborate hats. It is most often seen in the French Provincial style.

Bonnet top The top of a tall cabinet, rounded like a woman's bonnet; also called "hooded top."

Bracket foot   A base and foot treatment popular on English and American eighteenth-century furniture. When viewed in profile, the foot resembles the projecting side of a bracket. The diagonal inside edge of the bracket foot is often decoratively carved or scalloped.

Breakfront   A large cabinet, intended for the display of china and books, in which the central panel extends out from the two recessed end panels.

Brocade   Fabric with a raised pattern, resembling embroidery, often used for upholstery and draperies.

Broken pediment   The top of a bookcase, cabinet, or doorway, shaped like a triangle but broken at the apex. This decorative treatment, borrowed from architecture, is generally applied to large, imposing case furniture.

Bureau   A desk with drawers. In England and America, used to refer to any desk-and-drawer combination. Also known as a "secretary."*

Burl   A decorative veneer of curly grained wood cut from irregular parts of trees, such as the roots or crotches.

Butterfly table   A small, drop-leaf table whose leaves are supported by a swinging bracket shaped like a wing or rudder. This table was quite popular during the American Colonial period.

Cabriole   A decorative leg on chairs and tables that is elegantly curved, flaring out at the knee, tapering in at the ankle, and ending in a scroll at the foot. It is a distinguishing feature of Queen Anne, early Chippendale, and Louis XV furniture of the eighteenth century. The form is thought to be an adaptation of a Chinese leg treatment, brought to the West by Dutch traders, called a dragon foot, in which a scaled claw clasps a pearl. See, also, claw-and-ball foot.*

Camel back   The back of a sofa that curves up in the middle, thus producing a hump. Often found on Chippendale-style sofas.

Candlestand   A small table of Colonial design intended to hold a candlestick. It was available with a tripod, a pedestal base, or with the conventional four legs.

Canopy   A fabric intended for use over a bed or throne, either suspended from the wall or draped on a frame.

Canterbury   A portable wooden magazine rack, often containing one drawer below a partitioned rack for magazines.

Capital   The uppermost section, or crown, of a column. It is the part that is used to differentiate between the various architectural styles of columns.

Cartouche   A stylized shield or oval or unrolled scroll used as an ornament and often encircled by a wreath, initials, as well as other types of decoration.

Caryatid   A column shaped like a statue of a man or woman. Originally a Greek motif. Male figures are also known as "Atlantes." Caryatids are found on buildings and also appear as furniture legs.

Castellated   A decorative motif of regular projections and spaces resembling the tops of castles, or battlements, and other fortifications. Also called "crenellated." In furniture, a pierced cornice* or gallery of similar design.

Chair rail   A molding installed around the upper wall area of a room or located above a wood-paneled section of the wall which reaches the level of a chair back. It was intended to protect the plaster walls against repeated scrapes from chair backs; also called a "dado."*

Chaise longue (French, pronounced "shez-long")   A reclining chair with a long seat or attached ottoman. French eighteenth-century types were often constructed in separate sections: a chair and matching ottoman that fit closely together, or two chairs with an ottoman in between.

Chesterfield   A sofa mounted on short, castered legs, with deep tufts, usually covered in leather, with back and arms of the same height. Chesterfield sofas, common in late Victorian and Edwardian times, have been widely reproduced.

Chest-on-chest   Two chests that can be stacked one above the other; the top chest is usually smaller. Chiefly English and American, dating back to the eighteenth and nineteenth century; also referred to as a "highboy."*

Cheval glass   Literally, "horse glass." A full-length swinging mirror suspended between two posts in a permanent stand.

Chiffonier (Although the word is French, it has become Americanized and is pronounced just as it is spelled, with the exception of a soft "ch.")   A tall, narrow chest with numerous shallow drawers of identical size. The French *semainier*, a similar chest, only has seven drawers.

Chinoiserie (French, pronounced "shin-wah-zer-ee." Loosely, "in the Chinese manner or taste.")   The term refers to a type of decoration patterned after Chinese designs which was extremely popular during the eighteenth century. It is also the name for a type of lacquerwork, also popular at the time which utilized landscape and figure motifs taken from Oriental screens and applied to tabletops and tall cabinets.

Chintz   A lightweight cotton fabric with a floral design that has been given a glazed finish. It is generally used for slipcovers and light draperies.

Chroma   The degree of a color's brilliance, intensity, or saturation with pure pigment.

Classic, classicism   Decorative treatments and details based on the designs of Greece and Rome, collectively referred to as "classical antiquity." Later styles of architecture and decoration inspired by classic designs are called "classic revivals"; they include Louis XVI, the Adam brothers in England, French Directoire, English Hepplewhite and Sheraton, and American Federal. Today, the term has also come to mean a work of art of the first quality or an acknowledged standard of excellence.

Claw-and-ball foot   The end of a chair or table leg which contains an animal's paw, such as that belonging to a lion, grasping a ball. See also *cabriole.**

Clerestory   One or more windows located near the top of a wall just below the roof line. The term is derived from medieval church architecture.

Club foot   A furniture leg usually ending in a cabriole leg, with a flat, rounded foot pad.

Comb back   A distinctive feature of a Windsor chair wherein the back spindles extend past the hoop to form a crest resembling an old-fashioned lady's comb.

Commode   A French term used to describe a low, smallish chest that contains either drawers or doors.

Console   A narrow table placed against the wall or behind a sofa. The term originally meant a wall table with only a front support attached to the wall at the back.

Cornice   The decorative top of a bookcase or cabinet. The cornice molding, also called a "crown molding," is an elaborate band at the ceiling line of a room. The term is also used to describe a framework from which draperies are suspended.

Coromandel   Ebony that is blackish and similar to rosewood in texture. The term is usually encountered in "Coromandel screen," a richly lacquered and hand-decorated Oriental screen, greatly prized as a valuable antique.

Costumer   A stand with pegs for hanging clothes which was popular in Victorian times.

Counterpane   A bed coverlet dating back to the Early American period.

Cove   A concave surface or molding used to join the wall and ceiling.

Credenza   A buffet or sideboard used for serving or for displaying silver plate.

Crewel work   An Early American type of embroidery utilizing colorful yarns on natural worsted linen. The design, usually consisting of a stylized tree-of-life pattern surrounded by vine leaves and flowers, is an imitation of the Indian tree-of-life motif. It was also a popular design on seventeenth- and eighteenth-century upholstery.

Dado   A chair rail.* Wainscot* paneling reaching up to the level of the chair rail.

Damask   A flat-woven fabric, usually of silk or some other fine material, that can be reversed to disclose a pattern on either side. The design is usually a distinctive, classical, and symmetrical pattern.

Dentils   From the French *dent*, meaning tooth. Equally spaced rectangular blocks, resembling teeth, in a cornice* molding.

Divan An upholstered couch without arms or back, often piled up with pillows. Its forerunner consisted of a heap of Oriental rugs used for reclining. The term is rarely used nowadays.

Dresser A term derived from the French word *dressoir*, it originally referred to a table, or buffet, used to dress meats. In the United States, the term refers to a chest of drawers with a mirror.

Duck foot The end of a furniture leg resembling a three-toed or webbed foot of a duck. Also called a "Drake's foot."

Ébéniste (French, pronounced "eben-east") The French term for cabinetmaker, meaning one who works in ebony. In the seventeenth century, ebony was considered the finest wood available for furniture; hence the name for a fine craftsman.

Eclectic Borrowing and combining freely motifs drawn from many different styles. In room design, it means mixing furniture of different styles and periods.

Encoignure (French, pronounced "ahn-kwahnyur") A small French corner cabinet.

Escritoire (French, pronounced "es-kree-twahr") A writing desk with drawers and cubbyholes, sometimes even containing secret compartments, the latter giving the piece its English name of "secretary."*

Escutcheon A metal plate covering a keyhole or serving as a backplate for a handle or pull.

Étagère A series of stacked, open shelves supported by columns.

Facade The face of a chest, cabinet, or building. An elevation. The fronts of large cabinets, such as bookcases, were often designed to resemble a building facade.

Fauteuil (French, pronounced "foh-toy") A French upholstered armchair. The sides are left open here, while those of the *bergère**
are fully upholstered.

Faux bois (French, pronounced "foh bwa") Literally, "false wood." Hand painting intended to resemble wood grain.

Faux marbre (French, pronounced "foh marbr") Literally, "false marble." A hand-painted decoration intended to resemble marble.

Fiddleback A chair with a splat* shaped like a violin, often found on Queen Anne dining chairs.

Finial An ornament or terminal accenting a post, a pediment, or a point of intersection on a piece of furniture. Most finials are vase or urn shaped, although knob, pineapple, and eagle shapes are also common.

Fluting Very thin vertical grooves running the length of columns or furniture legs, intended as a form of decoration. See also *reeding*.

Fretwork Latticework; a border motif of geometric, interlocking lines; sometimes called a "key" pattern.

Gallery   A small railing composed of wood or metal which is placed around the tops of tables, cabinets, or buffets. The furniture maker Chippendale used galleries consisting of wood fretwork.

Georgian   A style of eighteenth-century English furniture produced during the reigns of George I, George II, and George III (1714–1820). The term also covers Chippendale, Hepplewhite, and Sheraton styles, although these are better known by their individual names.

Gilding, gilt   A decoration utilizing either gold leaf or gold-colored paint.

Girandole (French, pronounced "zheh-ron-dohl")   A wall bracket or sconce, often with a mirror and a branching candelabra.

Gobelin (French, pronounced, "goh-b'len")   Famous French makers of tapestries and carpets, established back in the fifteenth century and still in business.

Gueridon (French, pronounced "gay-ri-dohn")   A small French occasional table with a top large enough for one or two small articles. Nowadays the term is used to refer to a cigarette table.

Guimpe   Gimp. A narrow flat trimming, often with a wire inside for stiffening, used as a border for upholstery or draperies.

Handkerchief table   A square drop-leaf table whose leaves fold on the diagonal, like the corners of a handkerchief.

Harvest table   A long, narrow table with hinged leaves shaped either as rectangles or ovals. The legs are generally straight.

Hassock   A cushionlike upholstered footstool.

Highboy   A tall chest of drawers, often constructed in two parts. The lower part consists of either a table with one drawer or a low chest, called a "lowboy."* The term refers to eighteenth-century American furniture; the English prefer the term "chest-on-chest."* Also called a tallboy.*

Hue   A specific color, such as red or blue. A tint is a hue with white added; a shade is a hue with gray or black added.

Hunt table   A semicircular table, sometimes with drop-end leaves. It was originally fitted with a pivoting device to hold wine bottles. The term is also employed for a small buffet or sideboard,* constructed a bit higher than usual, used for serving foods.

Hutch   From the French *huche*, meaning chest. Today, it is taken to mean a cupboard with an upper section of open shelves; also called a "Welsh cupboard or dresser."*

Japanning   A lacquer work process, in imitation of Japanese artisans, consisting of a building up of many layers of varnish coats to create a luminous surface. This surface was often carved or inlaid.

Jardinière (French, pronounced "zhar-di-nyair")   A tall vase with pockets or a stand for holding flowers.

Kas   A tall, wide cupboard with a deep, projecting cornice* and base ending in ball feet.* Typically Pennsylvania Dutch in style, it is hand painted with primitive designs of flowers and birds.

Ladder-back   A rustic chair with a back resembling the rungs of a ladder. Chippendale greatly refined the design concept in his eighteenth-century chairs. Also called slat-back chair.*

Lambrequin (French, pronounced "lam-bre-kan")   The drapery around the top of a bed unsupported by bedposts.

Lawson   A type of sofa with square outlines and low, square arms.

Louis Quatorze   French style prevalent during Louis XIV's reign (1643–1715), who was also known as "The Sun King." It is also the name for the French high baroque style.

Louis Quinze   French style prevalent during Louis XV's reign (1715–1774), which coincided with the rococo style and is synonymous with it.

Louis Seize   French style prevalent during Louis XVI's reign (1775–1793), which was marked by a revival of interest in classicism, a movement away from curves towards straight lines, a love of symmetry in decoration and design.

Louis Treize   French style prevalent during Louis XIII's reign (1610–1643).

Lowboy   A low chest or table typically possessing two small drawers projecting past a raised center drawer. The lowboy can either be used alone or as a support for the chest of the highboy.*

Marquetry   An inlay of contrasting wood into a surface veneer, usually creating a pattern of flowers or shells. Tortoise shell, ivory, and mother of pearl are frequently used. See also *parquetry*.

Marquise (French, pronounced "mar-keez")   An unusually wide upholstered armchair or *bergère*.*

Méridienne   A short sofa with one arm higher than the other; unique to the French and American Empire styles. See also *recamier*.

Mullion   Vertical or horizontal bars dividing the glass panes of a window or the glass door of a cabinet.

Neoclassic   Literally, "new classic," meaning a style based upon a classical model.

Ogive   A pointed-arch decorative motif.

Ormolu   From the French *or moulu*, meaning "gold work." The term refers to the applied metal decoration on a piece of furniture. Ormolu is a distinctive feature of late eighteenth-century French furniture, especially Directoire and Empire styles.

Palissandre   French name for rosewood.

Parquetry   Decorative inlays of wood veneers in a geometric pattern. Parquetry is characterized by straight lines, whereas marquetry* is usually pictorial and contains curved lines.

Patina   The mellowing process of wood or silver resulting from age and use. A fine patina is an essential feature of a good antique.

Pediment   A decorative feature borrowed from architecture consisting of a triangular shape, frequently found at the top of a tall cabinet, which can also be rounded or broken* at the apex and inset with a finial.*

Pembroke   A table with a single drawer and two drop leaves, now commonly used as an end table or to support a lamp. It was first designed for the Earl of Pembroke, hence its name.

Pickled finish   A whitish stain simulating the finish on old pine furniture which has had its paint removed, consequently leaving traces of plaster or lime in the cracks.

Piecrust table   A small, round table with a tripod base. The edges of the top are scalloped and raised like the crust of a pie. It is usually considered eighteenth-century English or American in design.

Pier glass   A tall, narrow wall mirror suspended between windows or in a narrow space over a console table.

Pilaster   A flat, false column, used decoratively rather than structurally.

Plinth   The planklike base of a chest which is solid to the floor.

Porter's chair   An upholstered chair with a high, rounded hood intended to ward off drafts.

Poudreuse (French, pronounced "poo-drerz")   A small French dressing table or vanity,* usually consisting of a folding mirror and side leaves which reveal cosmetic and powder compartments.

Recamier (French, pronounced "re-cam-yay")   A chaise longue,* or reclining sofa, with one high arm. The name is derived from a portrait of Madame Recamier by Jacques Louis David in which she is shown reclining on such a couch.

Reeding   A decorative motif consisting of parallel, half-round moldings; the opposite of fluting.* Reeding can generally be seen on the legs of Sheraton furniture.

Refectory table   A long, narrow table named after the dining room, or refectory, in a monastery. It has heavy stretchers close to the floor.

Rent table   A pedestal table with a round or seven-sided top encircled with drawers which are often marked with initials or days of the week. It was originally used by a landlord as a file cabinet for collecting rents, hence its name.

Rococo (A corruption of *rocaille*, the French word for "rockwork" or grotto, and *coquille*, meaning shell)   A style of architecture and decoration prevalent during the reign of Louis XV, which subsequently spread throughout Europe. It is marked by exaggerated curves and a total avoidance of straight lines and symmetry.

Rosette   A round ornament consisting of a series of leaves arranged around a center.

Roundabout chair   A chair designed to fit in a corner so that the seat is placed on the diagonal with a low back on two adjoining sides.

Sawbuck table   A rustic table with an x-shaped base linked to a wide stretcher.

Secretary (French, *secretaire, escritoire.**)   A combination slant-front desk, or drop-lid desk, and a bookcase top. In England and America, often called a "bureau."*

Semainier (French, pronounced "se-man-yay")   A tall, narrow lingerie chest with seven drawers.

Serpentine   A curved, undulating front of a chest or table. The middle part is usually concave and the sides are convex.

Settle   A wooden, high-backed bench designed to be placed beside a fireplace and thus eliminate drafts from behind. The seat sometimes contains a storage compartment under a hinged lid; also called a "box settle" in Colonial times.

Sideboard   Originally, an open shelf (or board) on the side wall of a dining area used for serving food. Today, we refer to it as a buffet.

Skirt   The part of a table located just below the top which connects the legs. See also *apron.*

Slat-back chair   Same as ladderback* chair.

Sleigh bed   A bed frame with a scrolled head and foot board, thus resembling a sleigh; typical of American Empire style.

Slipper chair   A dainty, low bedroom chair popular during Victorian times. The back was generally S-curved. So named because it was intended to be used while putting on slippers.

Spade foot   A leg whose end is shaped like a blunted arrow, or spade; commonly found on Hepplewhite designs.

Splat   The center board of a chair back, usually shaped or carved.

Stretcher   A wooden member that braces the chair or table legs; also known as a rung.

Tabouret (French, pronounced "ta-boo-ray")   A low, upholstered footstool of French eighteenth-century design.

Tallboy   Same as highboy.*

Tambour   A sliding panel composed of thin, flexible wood strips mounted on heavy fabric, used as a door.

Tavern table   A rustic, low table, of English and Early American design, with simple, straight legs and stretchers. The form was used in public houses or taverns.

Tester   The top wooden frame of a four-poster bed which is intended to support the fabric canopy.*

Tête-à-tête (French, pronounced "tet-ah-tet")   A small, two-seat sofa or loveseat with the two seats facing in opposite directions so that the backs form an S-curve.

Thonet   A Viennese manufacturer who perfected the bentwood process and developed the café chair in 1840, one of the earliest successes of mass-produced furniture. It is still being made today.

Toile de jouy (French, pronounced "twahl-d'zhooee") A light fabric decorated with pastoral scenes or historical themes. It is generally printed in one color, such as blue, brown, or yellow, or an off-white background. It was originally made in Jouy, France, during the eighteenth and nineteenth centuries.

Tole Painted and decorated tin. Used as a base for lamps, on table trays, and on small boxes.

Torchère (French, pronounced "tor-chair") A floor lamp which directs the light towards the ceiling. Originally designed as a pedestal stand to hold a candelabrum.

Tracery A latticework frame for glass panels; usually found on bookcases and china cabinets.

Trapunto A quilted upholstery fabric in which the pattern is raised by stuffing the pockets with filler.

Tray table A small folding stand that supports a serving tray.

Trestle table In the Middle Ages, tables consisted of long boards resting on temporary trestle bases. Later, the trestles were joined by a stretcher and the tops were attached permanently. The trestle form consists of a base composed of two or three uprights which are joined by a stretcher.

Trompe l'oeil (French, pronounced "trohmp l'oy") Literally, "to fool the eye," meaning hand-painting that creates the illusion of concrete reality. Trompe l'oeil scenes range from realistically executed gardens and trellis work to false doorways, bookshelves, windows, etc. The artist attempts to paint the subject so realistically that the viewer is fooled into believing that he or she actually sees the real thing rather than the flat image.

Trumeau (French, pronounced "tru-mow") A combination mirror and painting fashioned as one panel. It is a typical overmantel treatment in Louis XV and Louis XVI styles.

Trundle bed A low mattress frame which could be rolled beneath a higher bed. This was a space-saving design of Colonial days; also called a "truckle bed."

Tuxedo A sofa with back and arms of equal height, thus giving it a boxy outline.

Valence The uppermost horizontal section of a drapery treatment.

Vanity A dressing table. See also *poudreuse*.

Vargueño A Spanish drop-lid desk raised on a stand or table.

Veneer A thin shaving of wood that is applied to a coarser, solid-wood core. Veneers are usually made of expensive, well-figured, and decorative wood grains.

Vernis Martin (French, pronounced "vehr-nee mar-tan") Literally, Martin's varnish. A process of fine lacquer work, imitating Oriental lacquer work, developed in France by the Martin brothers in the eighteenth century during the reign of Louis XIV.

Victorian   A period loosely coinciding with the reign of Queen Victoria in England (1837–1901) and marked by an eclectic use of different stylistic motifs as well as by many decorative "revivals."

Vitrine   A china or curio cabinet with a front door and sides made entirely of glass.

Wainscot   Wood paneling that covers only the lower portion of a wall, roughly to the level of a chair rail, with plastered walls extending above it. See also *dado*.

Webbing   Strong burlap strips used as a support for springs in an upholstered chair.

Welsh cupboard, Welsh dresser   A rustic cabinet with door compartments below and open shelves, or a hutch,* above. It is believed to have originated in Wales, hence its name.

Welting   A wrapped cord set into the seams of upholstery to outline or finish the edges.

Windsor chair   Early America's most common chair. It consists of spindles set into a hoop frame to form the back, a scooped wood seat, and four rakishly splayed turned legs. The Windsor chair originated near Windsor Castle in England around 1700, hence its name.

Wing chair   A large, comfortable upholstered chair with a high back and projecting "ears." It was originally designed to keep drafts away from the head.

BIBLIOGRAPHY

Ambasz, Emilio. *Italy: The New Domestic Landscape. Achievements and Problems of Italian Design*. New York: Museum of Modern Art, 1972.

Aronson, Joseph. *The Encyclopedia of Furniture*. New York: Crown, 1965.

Baker, Hollis S. *Furniture in the Ancient World*. New York: Macmillan, 1966.

Baldwin, Billy. *Billy Baldwin Decorates*. New York: Holt, Rinehart and Winston, 1972.

Baumgart, Fritz. *A History of Architectural Styles*. New York: Praeger, 1969.

Birren, Faber. *Light, Color, and Environment*. New York: Van Nostrand Reinhold, 1969.

Bishop, Robert. *Centuries and Styles of the American Chair, 1640–1970*. New York: Dutton, 1972.

Camesasca, E., ed. *History of the House*. New York: Putnam's, 1971.

Conran, Terence. *The House Book*. London: Mitchell Beazley, 1974.

D'Arcy, Barbara. *Bloomingdale's Book of Home Decorating*. New York: Harper & Row, 1973.

Debaigts, Jacques. *New Interiors for Old Houses*. New York; Van Nostrand Reinhold, 1973.

Fales, Dean A., Jr. *American Painted Furniture, 1660–1880*. New York: Dutton, 1972.

Fowler, John, and John Cornforth. *English Decoration in the 18th Century*. London: Barrie & Jenkins, 1974.

French Cabinetmakers of the Eighteenth Century, Connaissance des Arts Collection. New York: French & European Publications, 1965.

French Master Goldsmiths and Silversmiths from the Seventeenth to the Nineteenth Century, Connaissance des Arts Collection. New York: French & European Publications, 1966.

Friedmann, Arnold, Pile, John F., and Forrest Wilson. *Interior Design: An Introduction to Architectural Interiors*. New York: American Elsevier, 1970.

Gloag, John. *Guide to Furniture Styles, English and French, 1450 to 1850.* New York: Scribner's, 1972.

Grant, Ian, ed. *Great Interiors.* New York: Dutton, 1967.

Gregory, R. L. *The Intelligent Eye.* New York: McGraw-Hill, 1970.

Guinness, Desmond, and Julius Trousdale Sadler, Jr. *Mr. Jefferson, Architect.* New York: Viking, 1973.

Hicks, David. *David Hicks on Home Decoration.* New York: World, 1972.

House & Garden's Complete Guide to Interior Decoration. 7th ed. New York: Simon & Schuster, 1970.

Itten, Johannes. *The Elements of Color.* New York: Van Nostrand Reinhold, 1970.

Kirk, John T. *American Chairs, Queen Anne and Chippendale.* New York: Knopf, 1972.

Levallois, Pierre, ed. *Decoration,* 2 vols. Paris: Librairie Hachette, 1963.

Luscher, Dr. Max. *The Luscher Color Test.* New York: Random House, 1969.

Macquoid, P. A. *A History of English Furniture,* 4 vols. [*The Age of Oak; The Age of Walnut; The Age of Mahogany; The Age of Satin Wood*] New York: Putnam's, 1905.

19th Century America, Furniture and Other Decorative Arts. New York: Metropolitan Museum of Art, 1970.

Nutting, Wallace. *Furniture of the Pilgrim Century,* 2 vols. New York: Dover, 1965.

Sack, Albert. *Fine Points of Furniture: Early American.* New York: Crown, 1950.

Sharpe, Deborah T. *The Psychology of Color and Design.* Chicago: Nelson-Hall, 1974.

Shea, John G. *The American Shakers and Their Furniture.* New York: Van Nostrand Reinhold, 1971.

Stoddard, Alexandra. *Style for Living.* New York: Doubleday, 1974.

Whiton, Sherrill. *Interior Design and Decoration,* 4th ed. New York: J. B. Lippincott, 1974.

INDEX

INDEX OF DESIGNERS
AND DECORATORS